Fixing flawed urban planning
The case of Delhi

Other titles of interest:

Smart Urban and Rural Planning Techniques
Harmit Singh Bedi

Humane Approach to Urban Planning
Priya Choudhary

Geographic Information System for Smart Cities
Prof. TM Vinod Kumar and Associates

Metropolitan Governance: Cases of Ahmedabad and Hyderabad
Dr. Vinita Yadav

India's Urban Confusion: Challenges and Strategies
Edited by Dr. M. Ramachandran

Designing Better Architecture Education: Global Realities and Local Reforms
Dr Manjari Chakraborty

The Ekistics of Animal and Human Conflict
Rishi Dev

Water Conservation Techniques in Traditional Human Settlements
Pietro Laureano

The City Observed: Notes from an Unfolding India
Pallavi Shrivastava

Tirtha at Mukteswar: Architecture and Documentation
Dr. Ranjana Mital and Prabhjot Singh Sugga

Fixing flawed urban planning
The case of Delhi

Boniface G. Fernandes

COPAL PUBLISHING GROUP
Inspiring for a better future through publishing

Published by Copal Publishing Group
E-143, Lajpat Nagar, Sahibabad,
Distt. Ghaziabad, UP – 201005, India

www.copalpublishing.com

First Published 2015
© Copal Publishing Group, 2015

This book contains information obtained from authentic and highly regarded sources. Reprinted material is quoted with permission. Reasonable efforts have been made to publish reliable data and information, but the authors and the publishers cannot assume responsibility for the validity of all materials. Neither the authors nor the publishers, nor anyone else associated with this publication, shall be liable for any loss, damage or liability directly or indirectly caused or alleged to be caused by this book.

Neither this book nor any part may be reproduced or transmitted in any form or by any means, electronic or mechanical, including photocopying, microfilming and recording, or by any information storage or retrieval system, without permission in writing from Copal Publishing Group. The consent of Copal Publishing Group does not extend to copying for general distribution, for promotion, for creating new works, or for resale. Specific permission must be obtained in writing from Copal Publishing Group for such copying.

Trademark notice: Product or corporate names may be trademarks or registered trademarks, and are used only for identification and explanation, without intent to infringe.

ISBN: 978-93-83419-23-4 (hard back)
ISBN: 978-93-83419-24-1 (e-book)

Typeset by Bhumi Graphics, New Delhi
Printed and bound by Bhavish Graphics, Chennai

About the Author

Boniface Fernandes studied architecture and city planning at the University of California, Berkeley.

Former Chief Planner, Government of India, Mr. Fernandes was urban planning expert with the United Nations, Technical Assistance Programme in Saudi Arabia. His long urban planning career of over five decades has made him a well-experienced professional in urban development.

Mr. Fernandes has been closely associated with the School of Planning and Architecture in New Delhi, as a Member of the Academic Council and a visiting professor. He served as a Secretary, Delhi Urban Art Commission. He has authored books titled "Planning in India", "Making Delhi a Better Place" and co-authored book on "Design for Living".

Mr. Fernandes was a Member of the National Planning Commission's 'Metropolitan Transport Team' in the late sixties, and a Member of the National Commission on Urbanisation in mid-eighties.

He is a Fellow of the Institute of Town Planners, India, and served as the Secretary, Vice-President and President.

CONTENTS

Preface		ix
List of figures		xiii
1.	Morphology of Delhi metropolis	1
2	Socioeconomic profile	6
3	Beginning of comprehensive urban planning	9
4	Understanding urban planning process	20
5	Urban governance	32
6	How people in Delhi live	38
7	Urban aesthetics	61
8	Metropolitan transportation	67
9	Vision for Delhi	82
Epilogue		91
Index		95

Preface

Delhi experienced unprecedented urban growth due to massive influx of refugees from across the border, soon after 'independence' in 1947. Delhi could not be left to just grow, it had to be guided and corrected. Being seized of the gravity of problem of urban development, the Government of India created Delhi Development Authority, with the explicit purpose of guiding Delhi's development through the process of Master Plan. Since its creation, the Delhi Development Authority has three Master Plans, each with a 20-year horizon. The current one is 'Delhi Master Plan' 2021.

Unfortunately, these plans have not created any impact on mitigating urban crisis in Delhi. The metropolis continues with traffic congestion spiralling out of control, threatening to paralyze Delhi; overcrowded and troubled mass transit, eroding pedestrian life, and mounting parking woes; chronic housing shortages, especially for economically weaker section and low-income categories. Growths of informal settlements are rampant. That half the population of the metropolis, lives in unplanned areas, does not speak well for those who plan Delhi.

While most parts of the inner city continue to decay, the unbridled sprawl of the suburbs fill the countryside with mediocre houses, built and rebuilt, without any regard to the strain they put on traffic and other civic services. The spread out metropolis of Delhi is a least sustainable urban form, because of the exorbitant energy consumed by motorized transportation. The state of the national capital bears testimony to poor urban planning and lack of good urban governance.

With urban crisis looming large, there appears no will, no strategy, no priority and no direction whatsoever to the systematic response to the crisis, from those who plan urban development, and those who govern Delhi.

This book is about establishing what has gone wrong with urban planning in Delhi, and of fixing flawed urban planning in operation. In this context, it is pertinent to have an understanding of the metropolis of Delhi, as much as the urban planning process.

The book describes the metropolis through its morphology, its socioeconomic profile, the way rich and the poor live, its built environment, mode of travel, and the administrative aspects of urban planning.

This book is for the citizens of Delhi, with the intention of making them more aware and enlightened about urban planning and urban governance. Urban planning is making decisions that profoundly affect the form and character of Delhi metropolis, in which its citizens live and the manner of their lives.

Urban planning is as broad as the scope of urban government, which is closest to the people. It is an essential pre-requisite to the successful performance of duties of urban government, because it does offer most logical approach to solving city's problems, arising from rapid urban growth and expansion, as well as from changing conditions affecting inner city.

The 12th Schedule of the 74th Constitution Amendment 1992, inter alia, lists urban planning as administrative function of local government. For local government to deliver effective and efficient performance, it needs a supportive environment for which it must create condition for citizen's participation and engagement. The 74th Constitution Amendment mandates local government to form citizens' ward committees to participate in all civic affairs. This is an opportunity for Delhiites to be the change they wish to see in their metropolis.

The ineffectiveness of our urban government results from the apathy of ordinary citizens. The people who by reason of their prominence in business or profession, might be expected to play an important role in civic affairs, seem to drop out under the stress of political forces. Local government is then left mainly to politicians whose value and effectiveness in this field may not always equal to the citizens' need. In this situation, the importance of alertness on the part of the citizens becomes heightened.

Boniface G. Fernandes

List of figures

Chapter 1 : Morphology of Delhi metropolis

Figure 1.1 Shahjahanabad (Delhi) of the Moghul period

Figure 1.2 Lutyens Delhi – an imperial island

Chapter 6 : How people in Delhi live

Figure 6.1 Planned residential area

Figure 6.2 Planned residential area

Figure 6.3 Land subdivision regulation

Figure 6.4 Land subdivision regulation

Chapter 8 : Metropolitan transportation

Figure 8.1 Delhi witnesses some of the worst urban ills due to haphazard and tremendous growth of the city. Traffic snarls are everday occurrences in the crowded ITO area of the city.

Figure 8.2 Even in a place like connaught place, which was well planned, design has gone for a toss as burgeoning buildings, each accommodating hundreds of people, have thrown all traffic out of gare.

Figure 8.3 Types of motor vehicles in Delhi as percentage (%) share

Chapter 1
Morphology of Delhi metropolis

Delhi is a unique metropolis. It has an ancient history of splendour and squalor, of destruction and persistent reconstruction. The environs of Delhi are the graveyards of the generations past. Here numerous dynasties rose, ruled and perished. The Delhi of today is the ninth in the series of capital building. Delhi has become unique in other ways. It is a mosaic of diverse settlements, quite separate in character, origin and to a large extent in function. It's a collection of period pieces.

Placed at the heart of the metropolis is the walled city of Delhi, built by the emperor Shahjahan, in mid-seventeenth century. The medieval city is organic in form, its layout being natural than manmade. The streets are narrow and rarely straight, winding sinuously throughout the city.

The Chandni Chowk, a former imperial avenue, connecting the Red Fort and Fathehpuri Mosque, where the Moghal Emperor Shahjahan once rode, is today a hub of bustling commercial activity. The old havelis which line the side lanes of Chandni Chowk are of architectural significance.

In contrast to the pattern of the indigenous urban settlement, Delhi has the Civil Lines to the north of the walled city and the

British Military Cantonment laid out on preconceived plan, with defined functional areas.

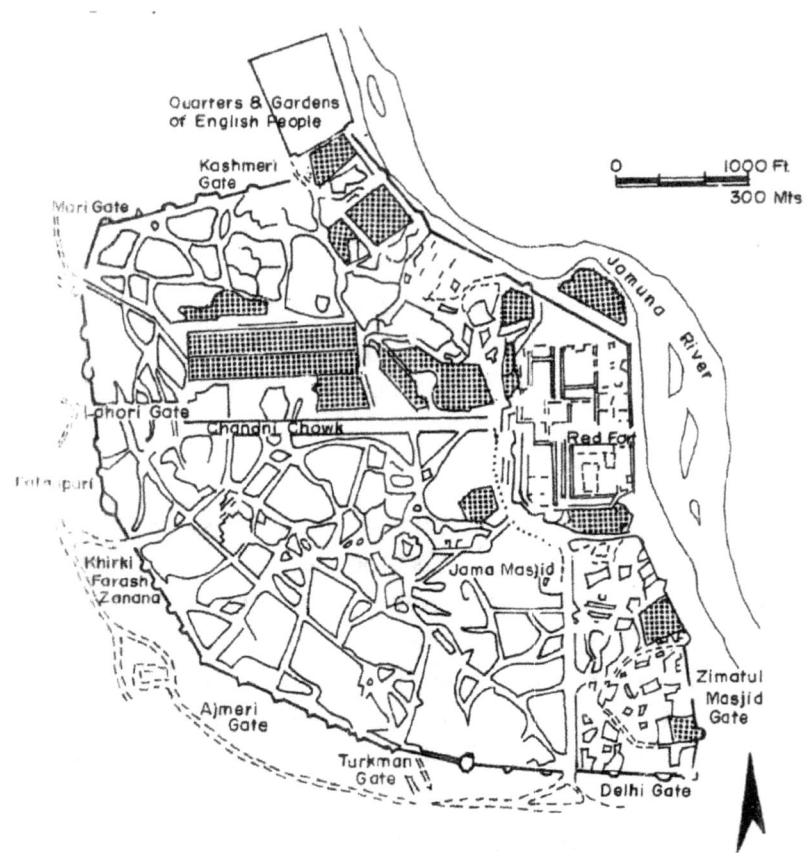

Figure 1.1 Shahjahanabad (Delhi) of the Moghul period

To the south of the walled city is the prestigious and pretentious official New Delhi, designed by the British Architect Sir Edwin Lutyen in 1911. Lutyen, who loved grand gestures and classic design, eventually got to put into effect his urban design for the imperial capital. New Delhi is geometrical, predetermined and ordered layout of city in sharp contrast to the walled city of Delhi. Symbolically, an imperialistic design the capital has a great East-West processional way: the Rajpath leading to Rai Sinha Hill, on which sits the Domed Rashtrapathi Bhawan, earlier the Viceroy's residence. At the lowest end of Rajpath is the magnificent India Gate, a War Memorial to the Heros of World War I. The area around it is the Princes Park, allotted to Princely States for building their residences.

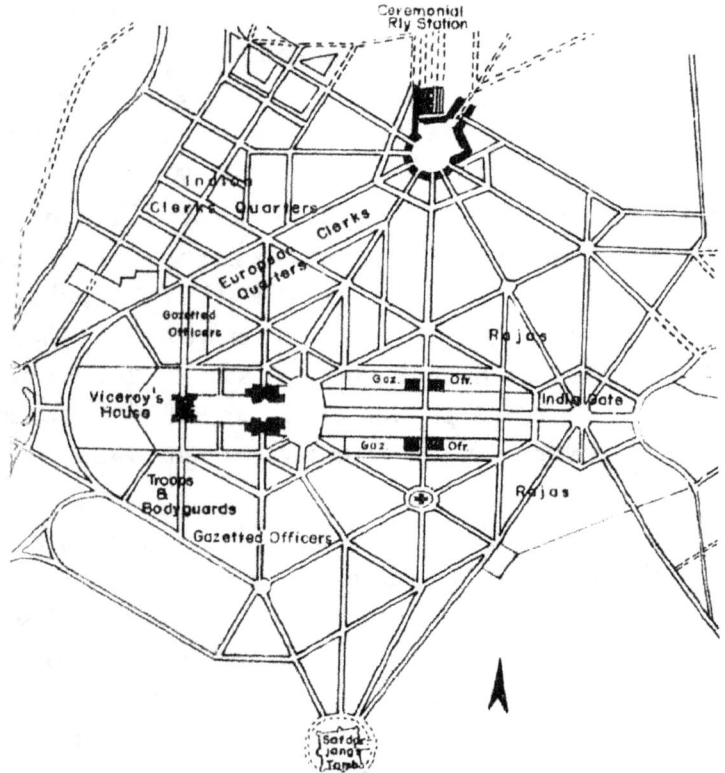

Figure 1.2 Lutyens Delhi – an imperial island

Lutyen's New Delhi continues to wear an expression of colonial grandeur, with wide tree-lined avenues, bordered by stately white colonial residences with large high ceiling rooms, colonnaded verandas and spacious gardens. New Delhi's plan is basically geometric in pattern, incorporating modified hexagons, triangles, trapezoids and circles. The focal point is Rashtrapathi Bhawan and the Secretariat Blocks. The westernised Connaught Place Shopping Centre, which was then sought to keep entirely aloof from Old and New Delhi, came up at different periods. The metropolis of Delhi has a binuclear commercial pattern: Connaught Place and Chandni Chowk. These are supplemented by markets. Then there is the unrestricted accretion of shops along the main arteries with heavy traffic.

To the southwest is the Delhi Cantonment, characterized by a fairly regular alignment of streets and comprise barrack blocks with rows of living quarters, for the soldiers and their families, separate bungalows for the officers, hospital, church and officers' club, together with parade grounds and rifle ranges.

After independence as Delhi grows, it derives its urban form and addition of undifferentiated residential areas 'refugee' and 'others', without any philosophical guiding principles. The metropolis of Delhi has grown, guided only by individual enterprise and builders. The unchallenged application of the principles of Laissez-Faire, in the building of residential neighbourhoods, has led to haphazard and unregulated development, an urban development without direction or vision.

The notable fact about population distribution is the sharp density difference in core area of Delhi. The population density varies from 5000 persons per square kilometer in New Delhi and Cantonment to 25,000 persons per square kilometer in Old Delhi Area. The population densities in suburban areas vary from as high as 30,000 persons per square kilometer on east of River Yamuna to as low as 6000 persons per square kilometer on west of the river.

The greater proportion of the growth of Delhi metropolis's population comes from the migration from rural areas. Added to it is the population of villages engulfed by urbanization; about 0.15 million people live in them. They have preserved their rural character and culture. This is reflected in the lifestyle and attitude of the inhabitants in these erstwhile villages which are partially and incompletely urbanised.

There are a large number of squatter settlements, so ubiquitous in every part of the vast metropolis of Delhi. These are makeshift and chaotic response of rural migrants for shelter. There are about

800 squatter clusters with an aggregate population of more than 2 million people, living in filth and squalor. There are about 1640 unauthorised colonies housing a total population of 0.4 million people. Dirt, dilapidation, and lack of civic amenities characterise these residential areas.

The Delhi metropolis has become fractured and incoherent, without a sense of place. Delhi lacks basic unity of layout and has developed mostly chaotically, only sometimes systematically; it has grown enormously in area and population to challenge our concept of health, happiness and welfare.

Chapter 2
Socioeconomic profile

Delhi, the National Capital is the seat of union government. As the Union Territory, Delhi has Government of National Capital Territory of Delhi. At the local urban level, there are three municipal corporations: the North, South and East Delhi; the New Delhi Municipal Council; and the Delhi Cantonment Board. All these governments together employ 27 per cent of Delhi's total work force, including health and education.

The economic conditions in Delhi changed dramatically, when India's economy was transformed from socialist to free market economy. Today, Delhi is the largest trade and commercial centre in Northern India, generating employment for nearly 30 per cent of the work force.

The monetary value of all goods and services produced (GSDP) amounts to INR 3657 billion: an increase of 687 per cent in 14 years. Delhi's economy is service oriented; the service sector contributes 86 per cent to the GSDP, where as manufacturing contributes only 17.6 per cent.

With just 1.42 per cent of the population of the country, Delhi contributes 3.87 per cent of national GDP. Delhi's per capita income is INR 2.01083, about three times higher than the national average of INR 68,747. Nearly 7 million people living in squatter settlements and urbanised villages are Delhi's economic resource. Hawkers and peddlers of goods in the streets are not accounted for in official employment statistics. But they are part of the informal sector of the economy. Just as they build their own homes, street vendors are creating jobs.

Delhi metropolis has 4.48 million houses of which 68 per cent are occupied by owners and 28 per cent are rented. About 61 per cent households live in one- and two-room units; 20 per cent in three-room units; and 10 per cent in four-room units. About 99 per cent households have electricity and 82 per cent have piped water supply. Every fifth household in Delhi owns a car. About 38 per cent of the households have motorcycles/scooters, and 31 per cent households have bicycles. About 86 per cent of Delhiites are literate. State government's expenditure on education is dismal 1.6 per cent of the GSDP and per capita expenditure on education amounts to a paltry INR 2,969. The expenditure on healthcare is around 1.5 per cent of GSDP. There is huge shortfall in hospital beds; with only 2.55 beds for 1000 population, half the number recommended by the World Health Organisation. Private hospitals provide 40 per cent of the hospital beds, whereas central and state governments together provide 38 per cent.

Only 25 per cent of the population of Delhi metropolis lived in planned areas. The rest of the population lives in squatter settlements, urbanised villages and unauthorised colonies; making Delhi a divided metropolis, one for the rich and other for the urban poor.

Delhi is faced with a dilemma. On the one hand, unskilled migrants drawn to the metropolis, occupy mostly public land, put demands on civic services, but contribute nothing to local government's revenues. On the other hand, economic prosperity has led to the expansion of relatively affluent middle class, which makes even more demands on the civic services. It is this class that puts pressure on housing demands that are often met by developers and builders. The windfall profit made from intensive use of urban real estate goes to the builders, whereas the unbearable burden of providing, maintaining or improving the civic services falls on the local government.

The Delhi metropolis is the engine of economic growth; therefore, it must be contained. Because after a certain level, the social costs of large urban agglomeration far outweighs the economies of scale. Daily commuters have to spend an average of 2 hours or more on their journey to work; if we compute the value of man hours lost in traffic jams, the human energy and fuel spent, it would show that the Delhi metropolis turns extremely unproductive after exceeding the limits of growth – the 'Urban Threshold'.

Delhi urban area increased from 22 per cent of state's area of 62.5 per cent in 2001, and population increased from 3.7 million people in 1961 to 13 million people in 2001. The population density increased from 9340 persons per square kilometer in 2001 to 11,297 persons per square kilometer in 2011.

The success of city-building strategy suggests more consciously designed dispersal as the logical antidote for the over compensation. By building well-planned living and working environments in the National Capital Region (NCR), cities and use transportation to help disperse population and employment in preplanned partially self-contained towns.

Chapter 3
Beginning of comprehensive urban planning

The challenge posed by rapid urbanization with its concomitant problems is how to manage our growing cities. One of the earliest responses to urbanization was an attempt to regulate and manage urban growth through planning. The planning response to urbanization and urban development process has itself evolved, through several paradigms, from long range comprehensive planning approach to structure planning and so forth.

The British introduced town planning in India in the early Twentieth Century. Planning was then confined to drawing up "town planning schemes" on parcel of land, as a framework for residential development. Important in its own way, such a piecemeal approach to urban development had virtually no impact on urban development policies and programmes.

However, the need for conscious urban planning to improve urban living conditions in cities became apparent and urgent only after India gained independence in 1947. Delhi, the National Capital, was the first city to initiate comprehensive urban planning.

After independence, the urban population of Delhi rose from about 0.7 million people to 1.44 million people in the decade 1941–1951, an increase of more than 200 per cent. The growth during this period was phenomenal, since 0.6–0.7 million refugees from Pakistan migrated to Delhi, and also because of the massive growth of government employment, from colonial law-and-order state to the capital of a great country. The proliferation of foreign embassies, business houses, all this piled up on top to natural growth. Under pressure from the exigencies of time, many urban development projects to house refugees were done with little foresight and without any coordination. As a result Delhi faced severe problems that may have been avoided.

Union government appointed Birla Committee in 1951 on the working of the Delhi Improvement Trust, noticed that no single authority in the capital had a complete picture of any general plan; an inevitable consequence of the working of so many agencies in the city. Since there was neither coordination nor overall supervision and planning of activities of different agencies, the Birla Committee recommended the creation of single authority to plan and control development of land and provide utilities and services.

In November 1955, central government's ministry of health set up a town planning organisation, under its administrative control, to prepare a Master Plan for Delhi. Simultaneously, the Delhi Improvement Trust was replaced by the creation of Delhi Development Authority. Prior to the preparation of Master Plan, an interim plan was drafted in September 1956 to provide for the short-term necessities and also to buy time until the final plan was developed in September 1962. Delhi's urban population then was little over 2 million people.

Even in the face of tremendous rapid urbanization and the visible pains and wastes of unguided growth of cities, there were then no comparable comprehensive urban development plans in the country. It is a fact that every sizable city in the world, whatever the character or the dominant political and economic system of the country, has made and is constantly updating urban plans.

The Delhi Master Plan 1981 with a 20-year horizon was a pioneering effort of preparing a comprehensive long-range general plan for the National Capital, by a team of young urban planners, with planning orientation influenced by education and training in the United States and England; Author being one of them trained in the United States.

Being the first ever comprehensive urban plan in India, the Delhi Master Plan became the pace-setter and influenced many master plans prepared subsequently for other cities in India. But experience has shown that this master plan approach had certain inherent limitations, which suggest that it was not the right one for the situation prevailing in Indian cities. One obvious fact is that it took years to produce any visible results, even in paper form. Delhi Plan took over 6 years, and equally long to get the plan sanctioned by the government.

Another equally evident is the fact that the Delhi Plan was prepared by an agency of central government, the Town and Country Planning Organization, with no real powers of effectuation. A third limitation is its treatment of single urbanizing area as an island, with little attention to national aspects or regional interrelationships, which may be particularly important in India, a country with limited resources and most of its urban growth was yet to come. There is also a much more fundamental difference between the West and India in the potential effectiveness of the whole "Master Plan" approach as a primary step towards urban improvement. Any such plan must take a great deal for granted to begin with, since it is essentially a method of fitting together a set of basic assumptions, the social and civic standards into a complex physical scheme.

In most of the US and European cities, these underlying assumption and standards were usually quite well understood, and therefore widely accepted. It is implicit in their plans that certain minimum physical standards of housing and services are both desirable and feasible, that growth trends can readily be projected, and that the established economic base will continue to provide both increased employment and adequate tax resources with little direct public intervention beyond zoning and services. In India these fundamental economic, social and demographic assumptions have hardly begun to be clarified in terms of viable urban standards.

We needed to ask ourselves: What is the affordable overhead investment per capita? Whatever the amount, how can it best be spent to provide tolerable urban living conditions. What should be the optimum urban pattern, from the viewpoint of social conditions, urban overhead costs, and maximum productivity, in variable local conditions? No answers to such questions were available to the Delhi planning team, and neither are they available to present planners. As yet there is not the kind of research, required to find real answers, is going on in India.

Delhi urban planners had, therefore, simply to make some assumptions of their own, which may have turned out totally incorrect. Yet the Delhi Master Plan 1981 provided a far better guide for development than none at all, and helped key issues. The specific issue that the Master Plan of Delhi 1981 addressed was the ordering of the future of the capital city for the maximum benefits of its inhabitants, as well as the visitors. The basic pattern of scheme of the Master Plan was to form all new development and reform old ones, on the basis of the "DISTRICT", as a relatively self-contained unit for daily purposes and needs, like employment, shopping, health, education, recreation and cultural activities. This locational relationship is of overriding importance in greatly diminishing the demands on the costs of transport and highways – both the capital as well as the maintenance costs.

The Delhi Master Plan was conceived to meet the following important objectives, namely:

1. The best possible location of employment centres and housing, by optimum distribution of work places, easily accessible to employees;
2. Eradication of slums and squatting and provision of adequate housing and related community facilities;
3. Development of adequate transportation facilities for moving people and goods and segregation of bicycle traffic from other forms, and especially creating separate bicycle expressways;
4. The rebuilding of deteriorated areas of the city, and application of effective regulations for new development;

5. Combination of utilitarian solutions to development problems with maximum of urban design for aesthetic effect;
6. Assignment of priorities to different projects, and preparation of a programme for their completion; and
7. Analysis of cost of undertaking the solution to planning problems, the sources of funds to carry them out, and the phasing and scheduling of the work by fiscal programme and capital budgeting.

One of the principles of the Delhi Plan was that besides being technically skillful, it had to have character to combine in modern terms, characteristics of a symbolic and cultural centre – the Heart of a Great Nation and the work-a-day metropolis.

One of the objectives of the Plan was to combine utilitarian solutions to city development problems, with the maximum of urban design for aesthetic effects. A great capital, New Delhi, deserves great architecture, or the maximum of which a generation is capable. This it has not been getting in its individual buildings, in its housing developments, nor has there been attention to the civic ensemble, the square, the vista. Opportunities are being tragically ignored. The Plan placed special emphasis on this aspect, not just verbally, but by illustrations and prototypes. This was fully presented in the form of "Ninth Delhi".

Having initially arrived at proposals for these needs in the Master Plan, the Master Plan studies should have been continued and actual conditions checked against the projection of the Plan. Continued study and thought ought to have been directed towards further planning, partly to keep in motion the implementation of the Master Plan, and partly to make any adjustments that become necessary as new factors emerged to affect the city.

Delhi Master Plan 1981 was based on detail analysis from which major principles and proposals guiding the future growth of Delhi were developed. This general frame work was supplemented by specific proposals for selected parts of Delhi. The prototype solutions to problems of various sorts with suitable modifications and consistent with sound planning were to be applied to all other areas so that as resources became available, development and redevelopment could take place in a rational manner.

The Master Plan emphasized that a balanced, comprehensive urban development is impossible to achieve unless all the objectives were met. Great care had to be exercised to make sure that those objectives, with highest priority, were so phased in their implementation that they were consistent with financial and other resources that could be made available.

Urban planning being a state subject, as per the Constitution of India, the draft Master Plan for Delhi had to be passed on to the Delhi Development Authority, in the first instance of getting the Plan sanctioned and subsequently laying down the process of Plan implementation.

Delhi Master Plan 1981 had clearly indicated a timetable of accomplishment and cost estimates for achieving within 20-year span, certain goals in housing, slum clearance, development and redevelopment, roads, public transportation, water and power supply. It also included land acquisition on a very large scale to facilitate accomplishment of these results, and to forestall further speculative rise in land values, which would otherwise make overall costs prohibitive.

Urban planning without a reasonably rapid and comprehensive development timeframe is not a satisfactory process, since development is obviously the touchstone of realistic planning. The plan implementation process is engendered through the preparation of 5-year city development programme. The programme indicates the projects that are to be undertaken in the immediate future within approximate time, and cost estimates of the projects. It indicates the public agencies that will execute the projects within their purview.

The great benefit of programmatic implementation is that no matter how little or how much can be undertaken in a particular period, what is done fit into a long-term plan becomes organic rather than haphazard. Unfortunately the DDA planners instead of complying with the implementation process as laid down in Delhi

Master Plan 1981 chose to adopt an adhoc and piecemeal approach to implementation, without a timeframe. The planners were more focused on development controls than development per se.

In the operational or development stage, the original planners who prepared Delhi Master Plan 1981 should have remained in the picture, as advisors, as the most necessary and least difficult step in the effective transmission of planner's intensions, and as an assurance against operational unawareness or disregard. Deviating from the Delhi Master Plan 1981, both in letter and spirit, particularly with regard to implementation process, resulted in accumulation of problems to be grappled with. Not drawing lessons from the default led to snowballing of unresolved problems, in the successive Master Plan for Delhi. No plan can be deemed as final and no plan worth having should be allowed to remain static. Urban planning is accomplished over long period of time. Therefore, provision is made in the Master Plan itself, for updating information and regular review of the Plan as circumstances change.

It was expected of the DDA planners to review the Master Plan 1981, to identify where the reality differed from what was planned. The planners failed to evaluate why the differences had occurred and to indicate those aspects of the Plan that were clearly in need of revision. The feedback from evaluation might have helped in influencing policy and objectives for future development of Delhi. Not only this was undone, but even while formulating the second Master Plan 2001, the planners overlooked the shortcomings of Delhi Master Plan 1981. The DDA planners have unwittingly aborted the planning process; nevertheless continue to make futile Master Plans that have failed to address acute urban problems, which affect living conditions of the citizens.

As provided in the Delhi Development Act 1957, in order to guide Delhi's development according to a plan, the DDA has been producing master plans, the latest being Delhi Master Plan 2021. Despite the plans, nearly half the population of the National Capital lives in substandard housing in squatter settlements, unauthorised colonies, urban villages and inner city slums, in conditions that are a true insult to human dignity. They are the most visible and dehumanizing manifestation of urbanization.

The master plans have failed to address vexing problems posed by uncontrolled traffic gridlocks, parking woes, pedestrian safety and troubled mass transportation. These pervasive ills of the Delhi metropolis are not inescapable, the problems results from poor urban planning, lack of good governance and political will. Delhi's complex problems, which affect the day-to-day lives, have aroused public sentiments, making it virtually mandatory for Delhi Development Authority and local government to address these problems with utmost urgency.

Failing to address critical urban issues, the policy vacuum has compound the problems. Delhi Development Authority, created in 1957 for planned urban development of the National Capital, has belied the needs and aspirations of the citizens.

It's a shame that nearly half the population of Delhi Metropolis lives in slums in condition that are a true insult to human dignity. Chronic housing shortage, especially for economically weaker section and low-income group category, has led to proliferation of informal settlements. The so-called planned residential areas are fraught with traffic hazards imperiling pedestrian safety. Permitting high density redevelopment of houses up to four storeys has further intensified the problems of residential areas, resembling cloistered living.

Traffic congestion spiraling out of control, eroded pedestrian life, troubled mass transportation, and mounting parking woes, characterizes the National Capital. Delhi's traffic problems reflect not just poor transportation policy, but a deeper and fundamental failure of urban planning. Retrofitting the metropolis, to be environmentally friendly and sustainable, has been blatantly ignored.

The problems of sprawling metropolis of Delhi are gigantic and cannot be left to the hazards of solving themselves. The free and easy meeting of problems as they arise will no longer suffice; there is a need to look for solutions of current problems in terms of the predictable future. The laissez-faire approach to urban development in Delhi amounts to repeating the mistakes of the past, which stood in the way of change.

Experience shows the Delhi master plans, with their rigid land-use plans and development controls, are poor instruments for guiding and directing the dynamic process of Delhi's urban growth and change. Urban planners should have the wherewithal about the process and causes of urban growth and Delhi's economy and social structure.

Urban planning must go beyond land-use plan to guiding the very complex, interrelated process of social, economic and physical change brought by economic prosperity of middle-class Delhiites. Urban planning has gone wrong, because the planning system in operation in Delhi is at best fragmented, uncoordinated and at worst basically non-existent and anarchic. Planning is administered by a bureaucratic planning authority, a negative force with powers of refusal and delay, without any accountability and entirely lacking the will or the resources, professional and financial, to take creative steps to make Delhi and environment-friendly place to live. The peripatetic shifting civil servants, (the Vice-Chairman of DDA) concept will not, in this relatively new development arena, deliver the goods. Specialized knowledge and experience is the sine qua non.

Ever since the start of urban planning in Delhi, over four decades ago, there has been no review to evaluate its effectiveness; as a result there have been no reforms to ensure there is no gap between contemporary urban planning theory and practice on the one hand, and to perform the functions for which it was set up, on the other.

The archaic planning model adopted by the planners no longer works in the dynamic interplay of economic and social forces that define the contemporary metropolis of Delhi. There is a need to mobilize human knowledge to grasp the urban problems, especially those that affect day-to-day lives of Delhiites, and to analyze and understand the metropolis and its crisis, then develop right ideas and methods on how to resolve them.

Regional approach to urban development

Delhi has been allowed to grow without any control, regardless of elementary human needs, until it has become unmanageable. The cost of maintaining it is far greater than the city can afford. Delhi metropolis is an engine of economic growth; hence it should have been contained, because after a certain level the social costs of large conurbation far outweigh the economies of scale it enjoys. The daily commuters in Delhi spend an average of 3 hours for journey to work. The value of man hours lost, human energy and fuel spent would show that any such metropolis turns extremely unproductive after exceeding the limit of growth.

The Delhi Master Plan 1981 prepared in the early 1960s had projected the population by the year 1981. Of course, the year 1981 was not an "Annus Mirabilis" the population of Delhi would continue to grow. The makers of Delhi Plan had clearly stated that unless we plan on a regional scale, the immediate action remedies for Delhi would inevitably fail. Because even if we planned and built large amount of housing, supplied water, the power and the sewerage, we would have still failed to catch up, since the major problem that Delhi faced was migration of population from impoverished rural areas and small towns. Therefore, it was necessary to develop relatively self-contained towns to hold job-seeking migrants. The creation of these so-called counter magnets will raise the status and improve the position of a number of smaller towns on the urban periphery, which are otherwise stagnating.

The future development of towns will form an integral part of a well-thought out regional development. The more that development is tackled regionally, the less would be the surge of Delhi bound migrants.

Having recognized the need for regional development, the union government set up National Capital Region Planning Board, which later in 1985 became a statutory authority, with planning jurisdiction over NCR comprising areas of Uttar Pradesh, Haryana and Rajasthan.

Unfortunately, NCR Planning Board's Regional Development Plan did not go beyond the drawing board. As a result Delhi continues to be flooded by intending migrants. After the first Delhi Master Plan 1981, the Delhi Development Authority prepared two more plans, the Delhi Master Plan 2001 and Master Plan 2021. In 1981, Delhi's population was 6.2 million people; in 2001 it increased to 13.8 million people. The projected population for Delhi in 2021 is about 23 million people. In the span of 40 years or so Delhi's population increased by 17 million people, while the urban areas of Delhi increased from 447 km^2 in 1981 to 1,114 km^2. More than 50 per cent of Delhi's population growth is due to migration from surrounding states.

The unbridled urban growth of Delhi metropolis has created serious implications for the urban environment and the economy. The large and sprawling metropolis requires huge energy consumption, in turn causes ecological changes. The intensive use of fossil fuels leads to heating up the atmosphere due to carbon emission from motor vehicles, thermal power plants, solar reflections, caused by roads and buildings.

There is as yet no real awareness of the big social and economic stakes, involving or the urgency of the situation. The urban implications of population growth and migration, and the severity of the problem of urban housing, for at least a doubling population in 20-year span, are not yet adequately vivid; they are scarcely perceived.

The problem lies not so much in any inherent difficult, as in the fact that there are few precedents for the kind of planning and research that is probably required. Innovations will be necessary. The NCR planning suffers from the fact that a "region" almost by definition is usually an area, for which there is no effective government structure; with the result there are no public controls to assure implementation of the plan. Also, there are certain recognized causes for the failure of plans to develop and produce beneficial or optimum results. One thing is that they remain on paper in great measure.

Chapter 4
Understanding urban planning process

The prime objective of urban planning is to create safe, healthy, convenient, and enjoyable place for citizens to: live in, have employment, bring up families, have privacy, and have community contacts. Planning starts with the people, and is for the people.

For existing cities, urban planning is occupied mainly with correcting the consequences of city's past growth replanning, and guiding existing and future development.

Urban planning is an intelligent forethought looking at possible future and making rational adjustments to or controlling the eventualities that arise. In today's context, urban planning must be seen as a dynamic, adaptive, iterative and continuous process of anticipating, planning and managing social and economic change.

Urban planning is not an event coming to a halt with making of a master plan as an end product. There is this notion that urban planning is a one-shot effort and that the master plan is a static event, a single elaborate blue print once and for all. Urban planning is a continuous and seamless process of plan making, plan sanctioning and plan implementation.

In the urban planning field, a systematic process has developed. The process is based on the fact that every agency, department or organisation in the city or metropolis, whose activity significantly affects development, is in effect a plan-making body, and has a vital role in urban planning process. So also is the citizens' role, since planning is their concern.

For its own activities, each of these agencies assesses its own resources and projects, its services and improvement and development programmes. Plan making by them has certain advantages, because it is done by experts in the techniques of the agency's programmes and is undertaken in close awareness of the needs of the agency. It tends to be practical, since it is usually influenced by awareness of the problems of implementation.

However, such plan preparation is by itself inadequate for dealing with the complex problems of urban development as a whole. Necessarily, each agency plans only for its own functions. Furthermore, single agency lacks the authority to influence the plans of other agencies. Some of them may not even have the staff or resources to prepare long-range plans.

This underscores the fact that technical expertise does not necessarily imply planning expertise also. Consequently, planning by these agencies has to be accompanied by plan making at higher level, with centralised coordination, that provides a framework within which all public agencies in the city operate and which embodies programmes or action that are realistic in terms of resource availability.

The next stage of urban planning process is plan sanctioning; however, the draft of master plan, before the finalisation, is published for eliciting public opinion of the plan, subsequent to which plan is finalised for obtaining sanction from the city council. Once sanctioned, the plan comes into force and is all set for implementation.

Urban planning without a reasonably comprehensive development timeframe is not a satisfactory process; because development is obviously the touchstone of realistic planning. The viability of the plan depends on its being translated into programme. The Master Plan proposals cannot possibly be implemented all at once; they have to be done in a phased manner, through preparation of 5-year city development programme with corresponding capital budget.

The programme indicates projects to be undertaking, public agency in whose purview the specific project falls, approximate time and cost estimates of the project. The vesting of capital budgeting function with the urban planning organization is the only dependable way of ensuring coordination among public agencies, thereby achieving targets and objectives of the plan.

Urban planning, by its very nature, is as broad as the scope of local urban government. It is an essential prerequisite to the successful performance of all duties of the local government. The Master Plan, no matter how well conceived, is worthless unless it influences official action. Therefore, it requires the confidence and goodwill of those who decide public policy at local level.

Ever since the British introduced town planning in India in early 1920s, it has always been the administrative function of local municipal government. With the emergence of urban planning as a pronounced feature of city governments, a planning agency, the Delhi Development Authority, working apart from the local government of civic affairs, was an addition to the multiplicity of local government bodies. Today, there are three statutory boards controlling electricity, water supply and sewage disposal, public transport and the DDA. Where the growth of Delhi metropolis makes artificial barriers of administrative control utterly unrealistic, the perpetuation of multiple agencies create one more problem for the planner, the executor and the administrator.

Experience has shown that the Delhi Development Authority as an urban planning body has not been an effective instrument for serving the continuously changing needs of Delhi and its people. It has not been responsive to local needs and conditions. Besides it is not answerable, as it is non-representative in character. It has not only weakened Delhi's local government functionally and financially, but it itself has fallen short of its potential and usefulness as a planning authority. Only a strong local government for Delhi can ensure that the needs, social priorities and environmental conditions in Delhi are reflected in local plans for urban development. However, local governments have not been given the political power, decision-making capacity and access to revenues needed to carry out their functions.

The 74th Constitution Amendment 1992 is about devolution of powers and responsibilities to municipal governments. Besides providing civic services such as water, sewage disposal and electricity for welfare of the citizens, the municipal governments are now required to undertake urban planning, regulation of land use, urban development and planning for economic and social development.

The present structure of local urban government does not have the political power, decision-making capacity and access to revenues needed to carry out the functions listed in the 12th Schedule of the Amendment. Neither does it have the expertise, authority and credibility needed to deal with these issues.

To be the key agent of development, the present local government set up has to shift to a metropolitan level of self-government, with enhanced political institutional and financial capacity, and more access to the wealth generated by the Delhi metropolis. Only then can the metropolitan government adapt and deploy some of the vast array of tools available to address urban problems.

The complexity and dimensions of problems of the metropolis are too formidable to be tackled through existing planning process more responsive to the changing social, economic and physical structure of the Delhi metropolis; the planning legislation needs review and revision.

Urban planning currently in operation must shift its focus from the statutory power of long-range vision of the metropolis, to short-term management of the urban system. A system based on two-fold strategy: one that is concerned with policy planning, and the other with programme planning. Policy planning focuses on performance goals of the Delhi metropolis as a whole. Programme planning focuses on achievement of goals for specific functional activities or sectors or subject areas that are of concern to the metropolis, for short- and medium-range projects.

Urban development policies are formulated and expressed through a 'directive plan', whereas programme planning is done through preparation of 5-year 'execution plan' and annual 'action area plan'.

The directive plan, unlike the conventional master plan, is not a rigid design for the future; rather it is a flexible framework, in which both public and private action can achieve common objectives. The execution plan shows location of projects to be undertaken and provides guidelines for preparing detailed project plans. It lays down planning standards and urban design criteria.

The planning and programming of all development activities for entire metropolis, as distinct from only a few development projects, enables translation of 'directive plan' into metropolis-wide programme planning, corresponding to national '5-year plans' thus forming a capital investment plan, as a budgetary tool, which enables coordination and implementation of public and private sector projects.

The final stage of urban planning process is the 'action area plan', for detailed planning and implementation at micro level of projects for specific areas within the framework of execution plan, be they redevelopment or new development. Action area plan provides flexibility for accommodating short-term changes in the directive plan.

Land-use plan: An integral part of urban development plan

Pressure brought about by massive urban growth, industrial and commercial development, expansion of motorised transport, with facilities needed for these purposes, exert great strain on the limited land resource.

Land is the most essential and perhaps the most precious of all our physical possessions. It is a national asset and a limited and finite resource. As Mark Twain put it "they don't make it anymore". Land is a platform on which most forms of human activity depend.

The manner in which people in cities utilise land, the activities that proceed on the land, the structures that are erected to accommodate the activities, and the spatial arrangements of the activities and buildings along with the roads and open spaces, are the dynamics of urban land use, which are taken into consideration in the preparation of land-use plan. Land-use plan is a means of promoting the welfare of the city, by guiding its growth along orderly lines. It is a great step forward in imposing order to urban chaos.

The land-use plan indicates the location and amount of land to be used for residential, commercial, industrial, transportation and public purposes. The land-use plan shows existing uses, which are to be retained and those to be changed, indicating the future use and population densities. Understanding of economic factors that influence city growth and development is basic to determining areas of land to be allotted to various categories of uses. The land-use plan also shows location of community facilities, such as education, religion, health, recreation and institutional. It shows location of roads and highways for movement of people and goods, terminal and off-street parking facilities.

Private people and public agencies in the city engender urban development. They build most of the housing, subdivide land for the purpose, put up commercial and industrial buildings. That which contributes most of development of the city is what private individuals do. Thus, the major part of determination of the form and character of the city is in private hands.

Here's where the land-use plan provides guidance to the private developers through development control measures which regulate/ control the use to which land can be put to, control of building bulk and heights, the extent of plot coverage and density of population. The land-use regulations rest upon the principle that no person should be permitted to use his property in a way that may cause injury or nuisance to others.

When vacant land in the city is parceled out into plots and provided with roads and public utilities and services, it largely shapes the character of residential areas and indeed of the city. The city government has its only opportunity to obtain a pattern of development with which it must live.

Therefore, a proper regulation of subdivision of land is of fundamental importance in carrying out the objectives of the master plan. We have development control measures that provide legal and administrative tool for regulating the use of land and buildings thereon. Similarly, subdivision regulations are necessary to control the design of street network, plots and sites for community facilities and services as well as space standards and standards for construction of streets, public utilities and community facilities. Subdivision regulations lay down planning principles and space standards and procedures for the developers and site planners to follow.

No land-use plan, however well-formulated, can anticipate all possible societal changes. Varying combinations of economic, demographic and political factors ensure that major changes are bound to take place in our so-called planned areas; and it is clear that we cannot respond to these changes without an effective monitoring system.

Monitoring is essential for both implementation and for constantly updating the database required for making quick responses to emerging problems and new demands. Land-use maps have to be kept up-to-date, and land-use plans have to keep pace with the rate of urban economic development and in migration. So, periodic reviews of such plans are absolutely essential if they are to provide a dynamic response to a dynamic situation. As has been done in other countries, the classical approach of planning for a horizon of 20 years will have to be re-examined.

Plans have to be solution-oriented to current problems. So monitoring is best done at the local level where implementation takes place. Local planning authorities must set up monitoring and evaluation division. Monitoring and evaluation must become essential components of the planning process; evaluation is periodic and enables one to identify problems as they emerge, and enables to make appropriate corrections in the plan. It is extremely important to remember that plan implementation involves activity on the part of several action agencies. The planning authority should equip itself to coordinate the progress of these agencies, through appropriate management devices such as phasing, programming and budgetary allocations.

Land-use–transportation relationship

Traffic is a function of land use. Various types of activities in a city based on land generate different types and volume of traffic, created by transporting people and goods. This implication of relationship between land use and transportation is of great significance while formulating land-use plan for the city.

Urban transportation has to be analysed in terms of its underlying causes and the need for movement of people and goods in the city. These movements and manifestations of organised system of various activities in the city are land based. Land-use plan stipulates not only use but also intensity of use, and this cannot be done arbitrarily. Therefore, transportation planning must be associated with land-use planning.

Traditionally, transportation planning starts with existing land-use pattern or a postulated future one, and identifies the resulting transportation needs and effects. However, new requirements call for analysing the reverse relationship, i.e. a recognition that land-use pattern is not given, but rather, is at least, partially the result of accessibility created by the transport system.

By now, a considerable knowledge of traffic characteristics has been gained. Besides, there is sufficient number of trained transportation planners capable of testing land-use plans for compatibility with traffic generated. In essence, the exercise involves creating a balance between intensity of land use and the carrying capacity of road network in the city.

Transportation models are essentially mathematical formulae, which equate travel patterns to certain characteristics of households and jobs. On one side of the equation is the location of residence, shops industry and commerce, the other side of the equation indicates amount and mode of travel, which results from people going about their daily business. The activity levels are affected by the relative affluence or poverty of the people and the types of jobs they have. If any elements of the equation are changed, there will be an associated change in the travel pattern. Thus, these models help us to measure the effects of change and enable us to test the impact of varying patterns and intensities of land use on road network and transportation.

The daily journey to work is greatly affected by the urban pattern of the city, in several different but interrelated family and public budgets, and in productive efficiency. In a spread out metropolis like Delhi, it would mean covering greater distance to work and the government. More mileage to travel means shift from walking to bicycle, to bus, and ultimately to expensive Metro rail. Travelling by cars, motorcycles and scooters has been intensified, thereby creating congestion and rising road expenditure. The urban pattern does affect transportation needs, but it is equally true that transportation has a direct effect on the whole development pattern and on land costs and population density in particular.

The land-use planning strategy must be of balancing housing and transportation costs, by judicious structuring of land uses, particularly employment pattern, the residential pattern and the relationship between them. General types of employment pattern relate to location, such as central, dispersed, and sub-centred, in terms of their probable effects on residences and transportation requirements.

If employment is placed in central area of the city, the housing costs are likely to be maximised for those who live nearby outlying areas; while, transportation and housing costs may be relatively high for those who live in intermediate locations.

If employment is widely dispersed throughout the city, some people may be able to minimise both housing and transportation costs. However, scattering of employment centres is likely to increase transportation problems. The most economical pattern of land use for expanded city is a network of relatively self-sufficient sub-centres, each providing fairly wide range of employment and related housing. Transportation system is likely to play a key role in shaping such an urban pattern.

Retrofitting the metropolis

While it is necessary to plan the growth of Delhi metropolis, one cannot overlook the need for its reorganisation. It is regrettable that urban planning in Delhi has not addressed the problem of correcting the consequences of past growth. Reorganisation of the city core and its related areas is a key objective in any master plan. Drastic changes in land-use patterns and worsening of the traffic problems, since the existing physical configuration was structured, increases the quantity and complexity of functions to serve a much larger and more far-flung population and its employment, as well as has changed technological solutions, greatly increased congestion and noxious industries chock-a-block with residences.

When the first Delhi Master Plan 1981 was initiated, Delhi's population was less than 2 million; it's a metropolis of over 18 million people now. Delhi was mainly an administrative city as the capital of India. It is now a vibrant commercial hub in northern India. Delhi is always in transition. Changing ideas and changing needs from generation to generation necessitate corresponding changes in the urban form. Changes take place when the needs of its inhabitants change. Each generation of Delhiites takes the city as the previous one has transmitted it, adds to it, uses what has been inherited or newly built until that has passed the margin of utility and then replaces the outworn parts.

To remain dynamic, Delhi must be able to cope with the problems it encounters amid the on rush of population increase and technological changes. How does Delhi metropolis change its ways and take a new lease of life? Well, it has to be done through the process of "urban renewal", which demonstrates how the obsolescent parts of the metropolis can be revitalised through integrated urban planning and massive civic effort.

Urban renewal is a powerful tool for improving the environmental quality, and functional as well as economic efficiency of the metropolis. Urban renewal must be planned and programmed as an integral part of the Delhi Master Plan. Unfortunately, radical urban renewal has not been attempted in Delhi, even after five decades of planning. Urban repair that is piecemeal and halting changes to the existing fabric of the metropolis continues as a customary procedure. This is yet another factor in urban planning going wrong.

Traffic is a most serious, single problem affecting the daily lives of the Delhiites. Putting in place a system capable of coping with demands of urban traffic must be a primary feature of comprehensive renewal programme until the problem of distribution of residences and businesses throughout the metropolis can be grappled with as a whole. Any effort to reduce the problem of traffic and parking is likely to prove merely stop gap measure. The fundamental need is for controlling densities through effective urban planning, also by removing gradually from areas of traffic congestion the establishments not functionally required to be there, and by separating land uses that generate conflicting or mutually antagonistic kinds of traffic such as passenger car and commercial vehicle. There are land uses such as strip-retail-trade abutting heavily trafficked arterial roads, which generate traffic that is in conflict with through traffic, leading to traffic snarls. Besides, customer cars parked along kerbs further reduce the road capacity which is inadequate to begin with. The strip retail trade along thoroughfares, so rampant throughout the metropolis, is a non-conforming land use and needs to be removed in the urban renewal process.

The markets and shopping centres the way they have been planned are traffic hazards that imperil pedestrian safety; there is no off-street parking for shoppers, resulting in roads abutting the markets and shopping centres, being turned into parking lots. Retrofitting the markets and shopping centres is necessary to make them pedestrian friendly and creating off-street parking facilities.

The other projects for urban renewal are squatter settlements, unauthorised colonies and urban villages; together they house nearly half the population of Delhi metropolis living in inhuman conditions and devoid of civic services. Their retrofitting should be on the basis of phased rehabilitation programme. However, urban renewal must be planned and programmed as an integral part of a full-scale programme of the overall city plan and policies.

Such a programme involves comprehensive and creative planning for the city as a whole, consisting of designing for the future interrelated plans for population distribution, land uses, transportation system, and network of utilities and services, based upon sound evaluation of economic potentials of the metropolis. It also involves the comprehensive programming in time and space, of carrying out these designs through regulatory processes, improvement programming, urban renewal and other measures.

Effective cooperation of private and public action is sine quo non for a successful urban renewal programme. Because, neither private nor government can do the whole job separately. In the older parts of the city, which are in need of renewal, the building plots are too small and often irregular in shape. Comprehensive renewal necessitates the reconstitution of plots for rebuilding. The basic city layout is obsolete, the city streets are narrow and utilities and services are grossly inadequate. The situation is not simply conducive to private investment. Since the private developer can only deal with the building site or plot, he cannot solve the greater "area problem", as a result there is little opportunity for successful comprehensive urban renewal on a solely private basis.

Private enterprise or builders require city government participation and support through public assembly of land, through "town planning scheme" and other public measures to create the desirable new uses of land in a redesigned urban pattern. City government, on the other hand, needs private builders to develop the sites/plots made available, so as to create the new social and economic values, which are the goals of renewal.

That is why there is a need for cooperative effort between city government and private sector. Government alone can undertake slum clearance under appropriate laws, and rebuild according to an overall city plan, provide the essential public improvements like new roads, water and sewer lines, open spaces and other needed community facilities.

Private developers and builders are already doing the job of rebuilding. They buy existing old buildings, demolish and rebuild high value structure, which they sell for private profit. Therefore, the city government should go for comprehensive urban renewal, whereby the city reaps the benefits.

Chapter 5
Urban governance

Who governs the National Capital – the metropolis of Delhi? The question arises because there is multiplicity of authorities engaged in administering the metropolis.

The urban area of Delhi, which is the Delhi metropolis, is divided into three regions: North, South and East, each of which is governed by municipal corporation. The corporations are under the administrative control of the Union Ministry of Urban Development, through a directorate overseeing the working of the corporations.

The New Delhi Municipal Council, which has jurisdiction over Lutyen's Delhi, is a nominated body, jointly administered by the union government and the government of National Capital Territory of Delhi. The last in the series of local governments is the Delhi Cantonment Board, a local municipality, under the administrative control of the Directorate of Defence Estate.

Besides the five local governments, there are several statutory boards: the Jal Board for water and sewerage, Delhi Electricity Board for power, the Delhi Transport Corporation for bus service, the Slum Clearance Board, the Delhi Development Authority for urban development, and over and above all these, the Government of National Capital Territory of Delhi wields powers of control and direction. The five local governments are left only with functions of garbage disposal, street cleaning and lighting, construction and maintenance of roads and other public work.

During the colonial rule, the British created municipalities in cities for directly associating Indians with local administration. Grass-root democracy rests on the assumption that small political units being close to the people make possible the purest expression of self-government, wrote Alexis de Tocqueville, a Frenchman.

The city has often been considered the 'natural home' of democracy. It is a place where the citizens exercise their power most directly and immediately. The basic problems of the people are local in character and should be dealt with by local initiative. One does not see this happening in Delhi. But that should change with the 74th Constitution Amendment 1992, which is about devolution of powers and responsibilities to local urban governments, and about citizen's direct role in policy making and its execution. The amendment stipulates formation of citizens ward committees to participate in all civic matters.

The 12th Schedule to the amendment has listed, inter alia, urban planning, regulation of land use, planning for economic and social development, as some of the important functions of the urban government.

Most of the state governments have effectuated the provisions of the 74th Constitution Amendment. In Delhi, the amendment remains a mirage. One sees a fundamental change in Delhi's psyche. Citizens of Delhi metropolis want to be heard. A paradigm shift in urban governance is necessary to meet the needs and aspirations of the urban populace. The officials as well as the councillors seem to forget that their role in a representative democracy is to represent the interests of the citizens.

The existing archaic, fragmented local government structure is totally inappropriate to deal with the urban process. This has made it difficult for Delhi Metropolis to influence the direction of urban growth and to manage problems of a large and rapidly expanding Metropolis. Quality of governance is measured by management of change.

The appropriate form of urban government for Delhi Metropolis, because of its size and population, is a unified form of government with a federative structure of two tiers. The first tier is the Metropolitan Council, headed by Mayor-in-Council, the commissioner to head the executive branch. The second tier is that of existing five local governments, each having its own jurisdiction.

The urban services such as water supply, electricity, transport and fire service now under the state administration must be placed under the metropolitan government, and so also the urban planning function, now under DDA. These services are legitimate function of local government which are reinforced by 74th Constitution Amendment.

The second tier will be the various municipal governments to deal with distribution of civic services like water supply and sewage and garbage disposal, electricity, parks and recreation, education and health services.

The Delhi metropolitan government will have to play a constructive role as an agent of change and development; it should have a general responsibility to promote well-being and sustainable development of the metropolis in the interest of Delhiites.

It must provide strong and honest governance, sound administration and skill-driven culture. Public servants, both elected and appointed, should have an understanding of Delhi's core issues and their possible solutions, so as to meet the challenges facing the metropolis. They must create conditions for a wider peoples' participation and engagement of the civil society in the national capital. Delhiites, on the other hand, must become more aware and enlightened about their rights and quality of life. The 74th Constitution Amendment requires urban citizens' direct role in the policy making and its execution. It stipulates formation of citizen's ward-committees to participate in all civic affairs. As a local government, the metropolitan administration needs a supportive environment that should enable it deliver effective and efficient performance.

Under the changing role of urban government for the metropolis, a clear understanding of the managerial alternatives and of its capacity needs is necessary. The change in the nature of the responsibilities and the scope of activities to be undertaken poses a new challenge. Strengthening the skills to meet the new challenge is imperative.

The metropolitan government will have to put in place a monitoring mechanism to effectively measure its performance and use the results to continuously improve public policy and performance. Monitoring the performance of the delivery of various civic services as well as assessing overall accountability of compliance with legislation and regulations about urban government organisations and functioning is also required.

The traditional bureaucratic system failed to deliver the types and quality of services that Delhiites wanted. Interaction between metropolitan government and the various municipal governments, both elected representatives and employees and the public is essential. Interaction is a form of communication between local government and the public that can provide valuable feedback about peoples' satisfaction with the performance of and services provided by the local bodies.

To become agents of development, the metropolitan government needs enhanced political, institutional and financial capacity, notably access to more of the wealth generated by Delhi. This perhaps is the only way the metropolis can adapt and deploy some of the vast array of tools, available to address urban problems. In so far as the finances are concerned, the distribution of financial resources should not end with the union and state governments, but rather should bring within its orbit the needs of the local governments also. Delhi, for instance, contributes in large measure to the gross domestic product. Delhi metropolis is an engine of economic growth. If the union government apportioned money based on tax revenues, big city like Delhi should be getting a lot more money. The 13th Finance Commission recommended allocation of more money for urban local governments.

Urban planning as an administrative function of local government

Urban planning is as broad as the scope of local city government. It is an essential pre-requisite to the successful performance of all duties of the city government, since it offers most logical approach to solving city's problems, arising from rapid growth and expansion as well as from changing conditions affecting inner city.

Urban planning has great deal to offer in evaluating city's problems and providing direction for sound growth and development. It has a full vision for the future, whereas the public agencies in the city myopically focus on their individual problems and projects.

The dynamism of urban planning process and the effects of implementation of several ingredients of the Master Plan seem to point to the desirability of integrating the planning process with that of implementation.

A planning agency working apart from local government of civic affairs was an addition to multiplicity of local government bodies in Delhi, with the creation of Delhi Development Authority as a separate planning body, under the administrative control of the Union Ministry of Urban Development; the management of urban development is fragmented. As an independent statutory authority, it is only tenuously connected with local government, and therefore has not been really an effective instrument for serving the continuously changing needs and aspirations of the citizens. As a non-representative in character, it has not only weakened the local government functionally and financially, but it itself has fallen far short of its potential usefulness.

Unless urban planning is made an administrative function of local government, it will never rise above its present status. As an integral part of the local government, it will be close to the elected representative in the Council and Mayor, and where it can develop a close working relationship with other agencies and departments.

Planners must popularize urban planning and development, the complex efforts and techniques involved in this relatively new and unchartered field. In Delhi and indeed in India, the public must have an understanding and conviction that this new field is of vital and pervasive importance and urgency to the polity, economy, efficiency and social effectiveness of the metropolis of Delhi.

Chapter 6
How people in Delhi live

The Delhi metropolis comprises of different types of human settlements where nearly 75 per cent of its population of 18 million lives in shanty towns, urban villages, unauthorised colonies, resettlement colonies and inner city slums. The houses they occupy are substandard and fail to satisfy a healthful residential environment. These are parts of Delhi, where human values are ruthlessly debased under appalling and humiliating living conditions.

The rest of the 25 per cent of the population lives in planned residential areas, which are by no means eco-friendly. The inhabitants of the Delhi metropolis, except for a fortunate few, are inadequately and uncomfortably housed. Such a contrast inside the nation's capital cannot remain, as mocking to our aspirations, as it is at present.

Shanty towns in the capital

The most visible and dehumanising manifestation of rapid urbanisation in the metropolis of Delhi – the National Capital – is the large number of squatters, so ubiquitous on Delhi's urban landscape. There are nearly 0.45 million jhuggis (shanties) cluttered up in 800 shanty towns. Men, women and children are in such a living condition that could be called a true insult to human dignity.

Squatting is, virtually without precedent, humanity's struggle for shelter; public lands are the most attractive sites for the squatters. Unguarded and unused lands, like the lands served for public use, lands held by Indian Railways and the National Highways, are usually the targets. As the squatters continue to rise in numbers, their resistance to ouster grows, especially with the patronage of the local politicians for whom the squatters are a potential vote bank.

Since the municipal governments are unable to grapple with the problem, more migrants move in to take advantage of official helplessness and acquiescence. The local governments have brushed the problem under the carpet. Neither the Delhi government nor the local government have any policy as to whether prevent, control, contain, direct or assist squatting. A policy vacuum is certainly precipitating squatting.

Poor shelter, as poor nutrition, poor health and poor education is a consequence of poverty. It follows then that strategies oriented towards improving housing conditions of the urban poor cannot be divorced from strategies aimed at creating employment opportunities. To understand the problems faced by the poor, let us look into their employment possibilities.

Employment in our cities is a function of economic dualism. Two sectors coexist – one is the organised, modern formal sector, characterised by capital intensive technology, relatively high wages, large scale operations and corporate and governmental organisations. The other is the unorganised, traditional informal sector, economic units with the reverse characteristics, labour intensive, small scale operations, using traditional methods, and provide modest earnings to the individual or a family.

Jobs in the formal sector are beyond the reach of the poor, because they require literacy, skill, experience and a level of training which the poor find difficult to acquire. Therefore, the informal sector is a critical component in urban employment.

But very little is being done to promote this sector due to government's indifference; consequently, employment opportunities for the poor are reduced. Government intervention and support is necessary to assist the poor in increasing their productivity and earning opportunities. The fundamental consideration underlying such a programme is reassessment of the role of our cities in development process. Cities are essentially an instrument for providing their inhabitants with a more productive life. Urban poverty can be minimised only when cities are thought of as absorptive mechanisms, for promoting productive employment for all who need and seek it.

A realistic strategy in this respect must place major emphasis on increasing the earning opportunities of the poor in the informal sector, which has become an integral part of the urban economy and a positive contributor to economic growth. Government can assist the small producer and self-employed. After all the entrepreneur is an important factor in the economic system, irrespective of whether he operates in informal or the formal sector. The informal sector, which provides livelihood to the urban poor, for many it is the entry level into the urban economy, and indeed the national economy.

The informal economy is not the problem; rather it's a part of the solution. Street vendors, rag pickers, market women, and others really do contribute to Delhi's economy. What the municipal government needs to do with the informal economy is to figure out how to help it becoming more productive.

Neither the state government nor the local government have a great track record in working with the people in shanty towns. Squatter communities and street markets have developed their own cooperatives. In Mumbai, women in *jhopad-patties* (shanties) and informal market places have created shared saving schemes and joint insurance plans.

Elsewhere, mutual construction societies that share labour and allow them to build their homes. Each of these home-grown institutions offers an opportunity for Delhi's local government to collaborate with squatter communities to install health infrastructure and services, water and sewerage. Shanty dwellers poor health and their economic status, will improve, when local government and squatter communities work together to plan and implement and manage change. The local government in Delhi must see their most neglected and marginalised masses as partners with resources and capacities if they want to complete a meaningful urban revolution.

The rural migrant when he comes to the city, he carries with him the same desire for a piece of land which he craved in the hinterland. He may not be able to build the best house at first, but he has demonstrated in his squatter settlement that given a secure foothold and some assistance, he can rise to the occasion.

The squatter community – the urban poor – are doing their best to help themselves and are capable of building relatively better house than public housing authorities, and for a fraction of the cost of public housing. This is so, because in their villages, in rural areas, the construction of one's hut is apt to be a personal family or tribal undertaking. Almost every person, in order to survive, acquires the ability to erect some form of shelter. It is estimated that the informal sector provides almost 99 per cent of shelter in rural India through self-help, and about 70 per cent in urban areas. There is also a high degree of organization and consciousness of neighbourhood in the squatter settlements.

The squatters have unsuspected vitality, initiative and creativity in solving the problem of shelter. Therefore, they must be provided with a wider role in housing. Given help with layout plan of the settlement area and given assistance in proper drainage, potable water and community facilities, the squatters themselves often band together into improvement associations. They can then transform the shanty town into a vibrant neighbourhood. Provision of loans, land tenure (pattas) encourages remarkable efforts of self-help. Granting land tenure as an incentive to invest their savings and energy in their houses and communities would be of great help. Government intervention needed to provide only the basic services.

The strategy should be to create circumstances for self-help and mutual aid. The measures required are institutional action, such as public control over land and the provision of services, which the poor cannot be expected to provide for themselves; grant ownership of serviced sites on which families are then free to build their own structure, which will be on the concept of incremental house, with gradual improvement at the hand of the owners over time, rather than high and expensive initial standards. Shanty dwellers' entrepreneurial energy illustrates the upside of urban poverty. These ambitious people working hard are also benefiting from proximity to city customers in Delhi.

While we deal with the squatters that exist, we must devise ways and means to discourage squatting and control its spread. We can only ignore such action at the risk of a "shanty townization" of our urban areas. India has a new national housing policy, aimed at eradicating homelessness, curbing luxury houses, upgrading village houses and reducing overcrowding in urban areas, improving housing conditions of slum dwellers and squatters. But policies must get translated into action programmes.

Delhi Metropolis is neither full of poor people nor it has made people poor, rather the prospects of improving the life attract the poor people towards the Metropolis of Delhi. It is just a transitory phase for the millions who aspire to work their ways in life. Local government must restrict its intervention in improving the basic facilities available to them, like safe drinking water and sanitation.

Urban villages

With the urbanisation of rural areas of Delhi, a number of villages that have been there for centuries are now integrated with the Delhi metropolis. There are about 135 villages spread out all over the Metropolis, housing over 5 million people.

Despite being within an urban area, these villages continue to be treated as "Lal Dora" areas by the government. The "Lal Dora" came into being in 1908 during the British Raj in India. It was initially a red line drawn up on maps, delineating the village population from the nearby agricultural lands for revenue records.

In "Lal Dora" area, villagers can build houses without conforming to building bye-laws and set up certain establishments without the permission of the local government. The status quo continues despite 'Census of India' having redefined these villages as census towns, wherein 75 per cent of the work force is engaged in non-agricultural sector. Continuing the "Lal Dora" concept is an anachronism; it has led to substandard development taking advantage of the Lal Dora policy. The builders are exploiting the urban villagers.

The pattern of redevelopment in the urban village is dense, haphazard and chaotic and without any civic services, indeed a form of unauthorized colony, and a slum, with incompatible land uses detrimental to the inhabitants.

The counterproductive policy of the government has led to adding these villages to the slums of Delhi. The urban villages are left out of the so-called inclusive urban planning process. To the planners and those who govern Delhi, people in urban villages and shanty towns are uncounted urban masses. Planned urban development must include as redevelopment areas.

Unauthorised colonies

There are about 1639 unauthorised colonies in the Metropolis of Delhi, housing a population of 4 million people. The rampant growth of illegal residential areas on private as well as government land has been going on for decades under the very nose of the Government of Delhi. Developers sell undeveloped or marginally developed plots at low cost in unauthorised colonies with the connivance of those in authority. All these colonies are congested hubs of illegally constructed houses, some dense to the extent of 90 per cent built up area as against 50 per cent permissible. These sub-standard residential areas lack fundamental facilities for health and sanitation and the residents' crowd into small spaces, which fail to satisfy human requirements for healthful residential environment. The roads are so narrow that the Delhi Jal Board finds it tough to provide sewerage because there is barely any road space for their work. There are no community facilities like education, health and recreation.

Regularization of unauthorised colonies is a key part of the election strategy, to woo a large section of voters, by issuing provisional regularization certificates, just ahead of elections. The expenditure incurred on granting provisional certificates is an excess burden on the exchequer, since provisional certificate does not alter the status of the colonies, as they were not linked to fulfillment of norms regarding any basic civic services. Issuing provisional regularization certificates that have no legal sanctity led to wasteful expenditure.

The Comptroller and Accounts General expressed concern about billion of rupees spent by the Government of the National Capital Territory of Delhi for developing unauthorised colonies might have gone down the drain, as the regularization remained only on 'paper'. Delhi government's notification regularizing these colonies violated Honorable Supreme Court order making basic civic services like water, sanitation, drains and roads mandatory for regularization. Also, the state government announced regularization without clearance of layout plans of the respective colonies, change in land use and collection of development charges by the local government. Colony coundries were fixed without verification by Revenue Department. In the year 2012, many colonies on private land and 583 colonies on government land were regularized. In reality, this was never done.

There is no actual physical control over land by the authorities. The anarchic attitude to land development manifests itself in squatting and unauthorized construction which is sub-standard. This anti-planning phenomenon takes place in Delhi because of official failure to determined action. The so-called regularization is to gain political mileage. The urban planners must retrofit the unauthorized colonies to make them environment friendly.

Planned residential areas

Delhi's planned residential areas comprise inner-city housing, colonial bungalow area in Lutyen's New Delhi, union government's employee housing, private housing, cooperative housing and the Delhi Development Authority's public housing.

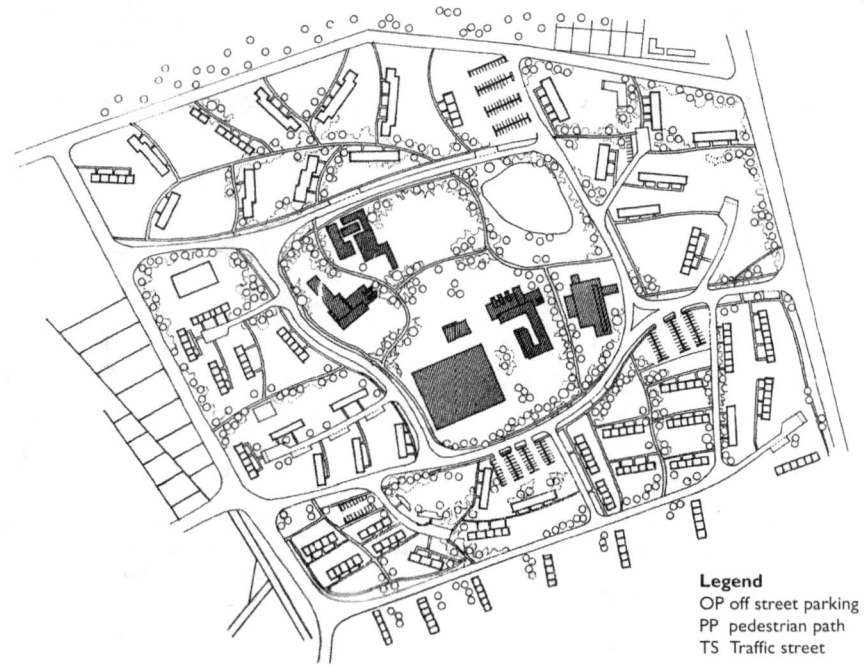

Figure 6.1 Planned residential area

The post-independence plotted residential development is mere geometric arrangement of streets and plots, with haphazard placement of community facilities without a thought for urban design. Irrespective of income levels, the residential areas are characterless, functionally a failure, with built-in traffic hazards, imperiling pedestrian safety. People live together in them but without a sense of togetherness.

Many Delhiites must have been feeling that the residential areas in which they reside, whose form and character they did not choose, but were imposed upon them by developers and builders, who have no recourse to planning principle or design standards for residential development.

House that an architect designs on residential plot is the basis of a home for the family. But a larger community needs a physical environment – indeed a neighbourhood in which there is space; opportunity for activities and a well-organised and efficient social life in which residents seek each other's company and contribute to the proper utilization of time in order to produce higher values of national and social culture.

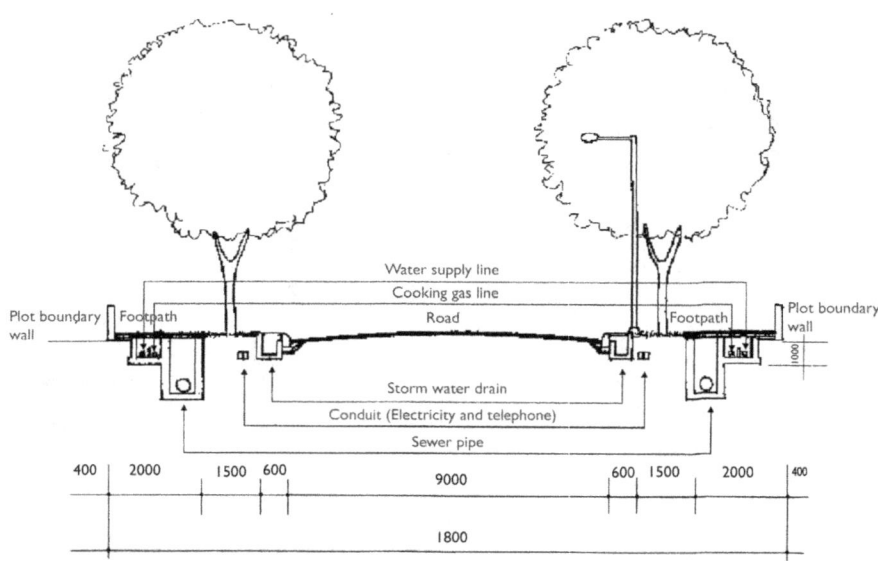

Figure 6.2 Planned residential area

The residential area should be planned as a physical and social entity, a more or less self-sufficient community with a definite boundary and certain required components. Proximity and convenience are primary factors in more of the activities on which neighbourhood planning should be based, like every day household shopping, children's education, recreation and health service, access to city bus and rapid transit or main urban highway. Every facility used by the people has some sort of "catchment" area – geographical area served by day-to-day requirements of the residents. Normally a 10-minute walk is approximately half a mile distance from the edge to the centre of the residential neighbourhood – conceptualized as the determinant of neighbourhood size.

Neighbourhood should be laid out so that in a few minutes residents can walk from their homes to parks, stores, services and other amenities of daily life. By organizing the neighbourhood on a pedestrian scale and making room for neighbourhood stores, services and recreation areas, local gathering places will have a better chance of coming into being. Today, walking within our residential areas is an exercise in courage. Motor vehicles zoom along the streets, sidewalks are non-existent; bicycling is difficult because the sidewalks where they exist are too narrow and streets are too full of speeding motor vehicles. We need pedestrian-friendly neighbourhoods in Delhi with wide enough sidewalks, so that people can walk without fear of getting hit by a car.

Neighbourhood streets must be designed with children's and pedestrian safety in mind. They include sharp curves and other traffic engineering techniques designed to limit vehicles to low speed and to prevent through traffic, which is so common in our residential areas. The pressures of urbanisation are eroding the neighbourliness and peace and quiet. We have to restore the peace and tranquility, which has been lost in Delhi's sprawling suburban landscape. We need residential neighbourhood, where errands can be made by walking instead of driving as we do now, where you know the neighbours up and down the street. All of us have that simple longing to mute the stresses, noises and irritations of our hectic city life.

Through the centuries, societies have spawned informal gathering places where the stresses of work and home can be left behind for a while. The companionship of others is important, which is instinctive to human nature. Our residential areas lack places where residents can go in hopes of striking up conversation with others. Sorry to say that clubs in some residential areas are more akin to restaurants for weekend entertainment and celebrations. As there are no informal gathering places, many opportunities for making friendships and pursuing common interests have disappeared.

How have the suburbs exacerbated the stress of daily life and what better alternatives can be found. People need a 'third place' outside of work and home, where they can make contact with others. The companionship of others is an important balm. It is instinctive to human nature, which we deny at our peril.

Our residential areas lack a physical core that helps establish their identity. The homes, shops and other public buildings do not have architectural elements in common, which make these structures look like they belong together. Instead the residential areas resemble countless "faceless" residential areas all over Delhi. Streetscapes in each part of the residential neighbourhood should be punctuated by focal points – parks, community centre, shopping, public buildings, which lend identity to each neighbourhood. The principle is that the foremost issue in designing a layout of a neighbourhood should be concern for the people rather than their motor vehicles.

Delhi's sprawling post-independence suburbs have no heart, no central core, no sense of place that residents can lean on and take pride in or turn to in times of celebration. After doing without it for 50 years, Delhiites must recognize and articulate their hunger for a public realm. We must together call for the return of a sense of community. We must make the developers, planners, architects and Municipal Corporation of Delhi, Delhi Development Authority, Delhi Urban Art Commission, answer the call in practical and innovative ways.

Sanctioning authorities in Delhi must accept only those residential neighbourhood plans, which are designed with sensitivity and imagination, so that residents can live in more pleasing surroundings, other than the non-discript, mediocre buildings, found everywhere. It is the lack of this kind of thinking that makes the residential areas in Delhi so much like a hundred other residential developments. The ugliness of the houses in which people live does not unduly depress most of them. They get upset or depressed on the issue of amenities like water, electricity than on questions of proportion and relationships of architectural forms.

Residential neighbourhoods are more than places to live; they are interactive components of a larger urban system. The residential neighbourhood is a fundamental unit of civic culture. Neighbourhood organisations, like residents' welfare associations in Delhi, should become an integral, ongoing and significant basis of civil life in the capital. It will be a community-led initiative to bring about healthier progressive Delhi. It will be like managing the city from the community base.

Open spaces

Requirements for public open spaces in residential areas have been reduced to a set of regulations that are primarily statistical. The requirements say little about the configuration and quality of open spaces. Usually, the main specification is a percentage of the site area. Since there is no stipulation about its design, developers distribute the required acreage from the residue left over after roads and plots are laid out, neglecting the fact that people use open spaces in specific ways. Precise standards must be established for the full range of traditional open spaces, so notably absent in our residential areas. Only specific standards will produce the specific open spaces that support specific activities. Without them, open spaces will only describe the dribble of green that is left over after the developer has finished laying out the plots and streets.

There is no civic life in our city. We are becoming an insular society. People seem to be withdrawing from public life into the shelter of their private homes. Many factors contribute to this condition. One of them is our changing physical environment, which has led to the perceived decline in civic life. Community cannot form in the absence of communal space, without places for people to get-together to talk and interact, socialize. Just as it is difficult to imagine the concept of family independent of the home, it is near-impossible to imagine community independence of the town square.

The vast Metropolis of Delhi has become depersonalised; hence, the restoration of neighbourly communities would tend to humanise it. The concept of neighbourhood reflects a general reaction against the monotonous and wasteful pattern of urban development. It's not only Delhi but all the cities in India have accustomed society to the paradox of collective living of separate and individualistic families. This has led to the habit of living together without the sense of togetherness, of concentration of people, without emotional integration. Sociologists attribute three basic factors to the creation of a community life in a residential neighbourhood: community consciousness, togetherness and emotional integration. These three factors together produce security and an atmosphere of creative and cooperative living in all pursuits of life. Such a philosophy must, therefore, dominate the design of a house and of the residential neighbourhood.

Revitalising neighbourhoods

How can we improve the character of the neighbourhoods, which make up the suburbs in Delhi? We need to fill in and heighten the quality of the places already in existence in Delhi. We should seize the potential of making the suburbs more satisfying. The suburban development has created a pattern of residential enclaves without the other infrastructure of civic life – civic amenities.

The residents feel that there is something wrong with the neighbourhood they live in, and also the whole physical arrangements of their lives. They yearn to belong somewhere to be members of real communities. But the feelings aren't moored to specific ideas about what it takes to make a good place. Delhiites should begin by understanding how much their environment affects their quality of life. Once this is recognized, it becomes obvious how we can best serve our own needs by improving the physical surroundings.

As a people we are not in the habit of thinking critically about our environment, or about how its form can dramatically affect the quality of our lives. Even a higher standard of living has somehow failed to result in a better quality of life. The residential areas in Lutyen's New Delhi have in some areas curved streets lined with trees. The trees were planted at formal intervals on all the residential streets. The formality of the trees connected the sprawled properties, and at the same time they provide a sense of shelter on the street – streets that invited walking. Compare this to our residential neighbourhoods today, where streets have no other function except to funnel the cars to and fro. We need to redesign the streets for pedestrian safety for making our neighbourhoods more livable.

Neotraditional development is the new interpretation of traditional communities that aim to conjure nostalgia for bygone architectural styles, for the safe and friendly atmosphere of small towns; where everybody can walk to school, to buy grocery around the corner, and to their house of worship. Individuals isolated from one another are powerless. Whereas individuals who form an active local society gain the ability to influence conditions; people coming together, discussing their concerns, exchanging ideas, noticing how the others respond, learn how to handle many situations.

Those who plan, design, build, and those who inhabit the neighbourhoods, should recognise quality of traditional design elements of mohallas/wadas that could be employed for society's benefits. The issue is not that in this day and age we should in every respect mimic/replicate the past. It is that our historic communities embodied many important understandings about human nature, about what contributes to a satisfying individual and family life and a healthy society. The past does possesses an accumulation of wisdom which we ignore at our peril. The development patterns of most of Delhi's residential neighbourhoods make for an inconvenient way of living, one that generates a variety of troubles for the residents.

A good residential neighbourhood must be safe, clean and have adequate water supply, sanitary and storm drainage system, reliable power supply, efficient telecom system; buildings there should conform to building bye-laws; availability of police and fire protection services and adequate garbage collection and disposal should exist; there should be access to good schools, primary health services, parks and off-street parking facilities.

Neighbourhood streets must be planned as a network of different experiences, other than just a system for automobile access to individual homes on the plots. Neighbourhood character comes from the shape of the street, the integration of parks and esplanades, and the different destinations visible on the axis of each road.

The neighbourhood plan must encourage people to walk or ride a bicycle; there must be vistas and architectural drama to keep the journey interesting; and the street environment should be designed for pedestrians.

The neighbourhood plan must provide community facilities functionally located within the residential area, so as to allow direct access by car, bicycle and walkers on pedestrian circulation system; and must create hierarchical system of recreational spaces in conjunction with educational facilities, so that their use in maximised.

We need to rethink our planning ideas – we need to develop suburbs that foster neighbourhood and public life. We must design suburbs in a way that public areas throughout the neighbourhood are enjoyable to use, and are treated as important, congenial places. Instead of glorifying interior and private spaces, while leaving the public environment dominated by ugly facades, we need to reorient houses so that they dignify and enliven the places, where residents come in contact with one another.

In the existing residential neighbourhoods, houses built on plots are being demolished and replaced with multi-storeyed apartments that behemoth as daunting as a cliff it represents a huge leap in scale. The old houses cower beneath the new comers. Allowing redevelopment at higher density on existing plotted development in residential areas, without thinking of the impact it will have on the environmental quality of the neighbourhoods, is a greatest act of vandalism.

In the process of redevelopment, the concerned authorities in Delhi have permitted four-storeyed buildings on plots in place of existing two-storeyed ones, without caring about the traffic chaos and the parking, which is already a problem and will be further aggravated with high density of population. Allowing four-storeyed buildings per se is not a problem, if such a built-form is in corporate residential development like one see in central government's employee housing planned and developed by CPWD.

The post-independence suburban development is the driving force behind the decline of Delhi's traditional urban and small city life. The suburban residential areas have no identity or a sense of place. We must call for the return of a sense of community in our residential areas. Developers, urban planners and urban designers must answer the call in practical and innovative ways.

There should be architecture that respects human scale, respects regional history and ecology. Traditional architecture has much to teach us about these imperatives, without prescribing nostalgic forms. Climate, responsive to design that honours the history and culture of a place, and combined with new technology and lead to innovative rather than imitative design.

Residential neighbourhoods can be shaped by choice or can be shaped by chance. We either keep on accepting the kind of neighbourhoods we get, or we can insist on getting the kind of neighbourhoods we want. It was Sir Winston Churchill who said that "we shape our cities and then our cities shape us". The choice is ours whether we build sub-divisions that debase the human spirit or neighbourhoods that nurture sociability and bring out the best in our nature. The techniques for achieving the latter are well known, and available to all who wish to make places worth caring about.

It is the buildings – houses – that comprise a place, and architecture is known as the art of place making. We have not shaped our place in Delhi, residential or commercial in the post-independence era so well.

Traditional residential neighbourhoods used to give the inhabitants a sense of belonging. Every residential area in the capital's suburbs is more like every other residential area, all adding up to no place. The built spaces of the city deeply influence the quality of community life; therefore, the urban planners and architects have the responsibility to design and construct the aesthetically pleasing environment for the citizens of Delhi.

We need a society of neighbourhoods, a culture of personal responsibility. Today not much attention is given to management aspects of residential neighbourhoods. Unless our neighbourhoods are permanently managed by trained personnel, the best residential areas could be converted into slums. Good housing management is based on a developing social consciousness. Therefore, self-managed neighbourhoods must be undertaken to provide for their own welfare, through active and sustained community participation.

The residential welfare associations (RWAs) need to play a key role in revitalisation of residential neighbourhoods and for promoting a sense of community, supported by national resources. Neighbourhood-based initiatives are important, because they ensure that the residents both initiate and support programmes for their own neighbourhoods. Chances for success can improve dramatically, when the neighbourhood community is a partner to development.

To make Delhi a better place, we the citizens must bring our new visions of development and policy goals to the local level, down to where people live, down to where they experience development, down to where people themselves take initiatives to transform their own living conditions.

Resident's welfare associations must be empowered as new players in efforts to revitalise neighbourhoods on the decline. A community development movement is necessary; a movement that involves citizen's participation, political commitment and government and private sector support for neighbourhood planning and development.

At the dawn of independence, Delhi's population was less than 2 million; today Delhi has 15 million people creating an entirely new scale of urban development, a scale that has changed the nature and character of urban form.

From the detached house, through semi-detached and attached row-house on plots to the apartment blocks and high-rise buildings, is the response of the inhabitants of Delhi to population pressure.

The problem of mega-scale is real. The land resources being severely restricted, high densities became inevitable. High-rise residential buildings are being super imposed on plots in place of a detached or semi-detached house.

To mitigate the chaos that has created as a result will require new inventions, new design methodologies, and unprecedented solutions. The architectural profession must rise to the occasion; the mega scale must be recognized as a paradigm shift that inevitably challenges the basic assumptions of architecture.

One of the most frustrating aspects of living in a high-rise apartment building is its inaccessibility to the outdoors, like sitting in a garden. However, architect Moshe Safdie's 'Habitat', which he designed and built at the Montreal Expo in 1967, emerged as a structure combining some of the amenities of single-family housing with the unique opportunities of a high-rise building. It substituted exterior walkways for interior corridors, shaping the building's mass to create roof-gardens, multiple exposures, acoustic privacy, and articulating the scale of individual dwellings.

As Habitat Complex was inhabited, a change in perception immediately occurred on the part of its residents: corridor became street, apartment became house and balcony a garden. The pleasures of living in privacy were added to the benefits of living in close community. Increasingly, in the core as well as the perimeters of Delhi, for the poor, the middle-income and the affluent, the high-rise apartment building emerges as the predominant urban form.

Land subdivision regulation

The cities expand primarily through the process of development of parcels of land. Land is developed by either a public authority, cooperatives or private developer, who markets the plots to the prospective users.

Every time a new land subdivision, with its streets, plots and open spaces, is planned and developed, a piece of urban planning and building is accomplished. Whoever plans a subdivision inevitably plans a portion of the city. The guidance of this development in harmony with city objectives is, therefore, a most important urban planning opportunity.

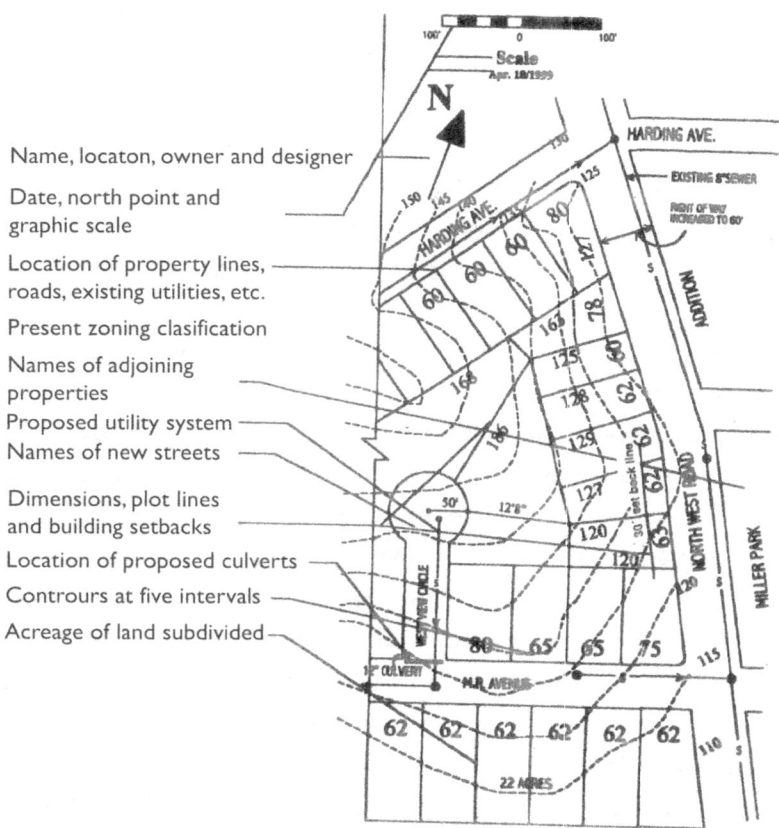

Figure 6.3 Land subdivision regulation

Since residential subdivision is the most common method of adding to the housing supply in the city, and since the need for new housing will continue far into the future, the subdivisions that are planned and created today will largely shape the character of the city. It, therefore, behooves the urban planning authorities to make sure that each new addition to the city is the best that today's design can provide. Regulation of land subdivision is the city's most important device for assuring that new residential areas retain their beauty and value. As suburban areas continue to spring up and expand, Delhi Metropolis faces vital decisions affecting the subdivision of land.

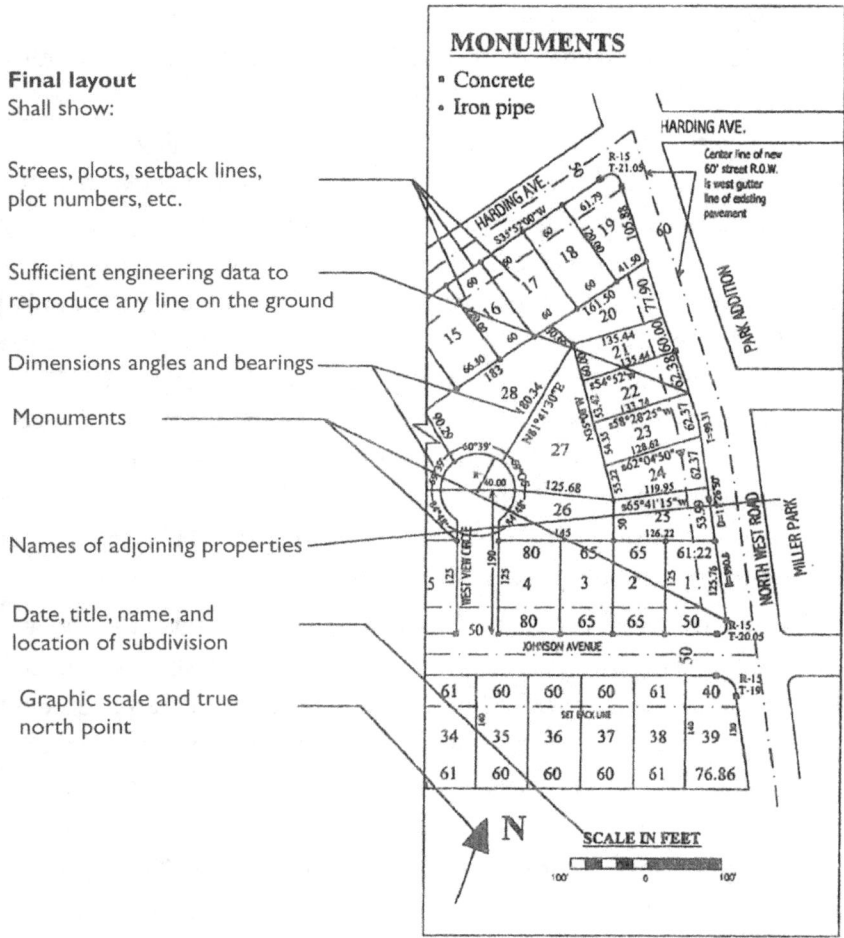

Figure 6.4 Land subdivision regulation

Land subdivision regulations are a set of guidelines for controlling the quality of land development by the urban planning authority. In its review of land subdivision layout plan for residential area, the planning authority checks the arrangement and width of streets for traffic safety, the design of street network, particularly as to its conformity with the major road and street plan of the city and standards set by the Master Plan, and also checks the depth and width of plots, the length of the blocks, the provision of open spaces for recreation, and community facilities, the provision of drainage, water supply, street lighting, the grading and surfacing of streets, and the sufficiency of easements for utility installations, street planting, pedestrian paths, off-street parking facilities.

The developer is required to conform to planning standards prescribed in a published set of land subdivision regulations for residential areas, prepared and adopted by the city planning authority. Along with the approval of the preliminary subdivision plan, the developer has to get the necessary permission from the planning authority for construction and for inspection of the work to be undertaken by him with regard to subdivision layout plan. Once the developer completes the construction work in his subdivision to the satisfaction of the planning authority, the developer has to file with the authority a final subdivision plan for approval. The final sanction is given only when the planning authority is satisfied that the developer has complied with the city's subdivision regulations.

While the town planning laws in India do require the review of land subdivisions before they are approved or sanctioned, the planning authorities do not have any set of published requirements to which subdivision of land must conform, and also make it available to the public. This would have provided the prospective developers with the knowledge of what is expected of them.

The regulations may not necessarily guarantee that all subdivisions will be of an equally high order of design, for obviously much will depend on the capability of the subdivision layout planner and designer. It is, therefore, essential that the developers, be they private or public or cooperatives, should be educated in good practices through the publication of brochures by the planning authority, indicating diagrams and photographs, illustrating model types of layouts and detail design as part of the subdivision regulations.

Residential neighbourhood planning guidelines in the brochure must ensure that the street network should be designed to accommodate only local traffic. Through or extraneous traffic should be directed around the residential neighbourhood along its peripheral roads, which also serve as the boundaries or limits of the neighbourhood, thereby increasing traffic safety. Parking facilities for the residents and visitors should be provided partly along the road curbs, but principally within a series of parking bays or plots.

The guidelines must ensure that the neighbourhood promotes independence from the motor car or any motor vehicular transport, by bringing the needs of daily living within walking distance of the residents. By reducing the number of car trips and length of trips, certain social objectives are achieved, like increased personal time, reduced traffic congestion, conservation of land and fuel. It promotes security through neighbourliness, promotes social integration of age and economic classes, by providing a full range of housing types and commercial opportunities. It provides education, health and recreational facilities.

The principal element shaping the spatial arrangement of the various housing developments in such neighbourhoods is pedestrian lanes or paths, lined on both sides of buildings. Such lanes give access to the basic functional elements of the neighbourhood – the residential buildings, schools, shops and service centres as well as clubs for residents. Playgrounds for children and recreational areas for young adults are spatially connected with lanes or paths. The concentration of most functions of the neighbourhood in the nearest vicinity of the pedestrian lanes with a distinct compact shape leads to spatial integration. Community facilities should be located in relation to each other, so as to meet the standards of convenient and safe access between homes and community facilities, to encourage the fullest use of all community facilities by the residents, to create a focal point in the neighbourhood, which will stimulate the growth of vital community relationships. Centrally located community facilities will serve as a focal point of architectural interest and residential activity.

Giving the pedestrian lanes individual features by means of differentiation in the forms of buildings, the facades will help to do away with the nightmare of many of our contemporary residential areas in the cities, which soporific vagueness of space that belongs to no one and is treated by everyone exclusively as a distance between the bus stop and the door to their homes. Separation of buildings, meandering, narrowing and broadening lanes, the undulating ground, small garden plots around the houses – all these enrich the surroundings of the buildings and relieve the monotony.

A skillful treatment of vegetation in the development of residential areas plays an important role – aesthetic, utilitarian and hygienic. In order to create a pleasant atmosphere in our residential areas, it is essential to provide some plant life that is visible from all dwellings in the neighbourhood. Besides beautifying, well-handled planting of trees often help in reducing the level of noise and also dust, to which the residents in our cities are subject to, and in the visual screening of objectionable structures or service functions and in controlling glare of the sun or night traffic.

Functional planning of open spaces and parks, in relation to the residential community facilities, can make the difference between a good and poor neighbourhood. The park system should be laid so as to connect with the other residential open spaces. It should tie all parts of the residential neighbourhood together in order to create a feeling of continuous open park space throughout the residential area.

This calls for skillful urban design by competent planners and architects, landscape architects, working in collaboration.

Chapter 7
Urban aesthetics

Urban planning is not simply a matter of allotting land for various kinds of development. It is equally concerned with the form of development and the quality of the physical environment. Ultimately, what matters is not simply where development occurs, its form and quality are equally important as our planning process will always be judged, in the final analysis, by the quality of results it produces.

Along with the more utilitarian features of urban land potentials, land-use planning must concern itself with the perceptual aspects of the urban environment, with its aesthetic qualities, and with the preservation and development of distinctive natural and manmade features. It must not be forgotten that the very origins of city planning and its early development possessed a strong aesthetic orientation, and that issues of urban aesthetics have for long been closely linked with the basic objectives of city planning. However, in the recent past, our pre-occupation with socio-economic and engineering investigations has led us to overlook the aesthetic aspect of urban development. The results of this neglect are all too apparent. Urban aesthetics must, therefore, be accorded a far more important role now in a comprehensive approach to urban development.

In his book "The Form of Cities", Kevin Lynch observed that urban areas possess distinct and recordable qualities that affect peoples' perceptual satisfactions with the urban environment. Several considerations determine urban form, structure and quality: the placement of key functional areas and buildings, the location of circulation routes, the sitting of residential and other areas with regard to key reference points, orientation, prevailing winds, existing vistas, and so on. A systematic study of these elements and their relationship to each other should be an essential component of the land-use planning process. Without it, creativity will be absent.

In his book "Urban Aesthetics", Sidney Williams has suggested a useful approach to studying the aesthetic characteristics of cities. The 'visual survey' technique outlined by him consists of two parts. In the first part, one identifies the three-dimensional characteristics of the city: site and the manmade features, which have been added to it. In the second part, one records significant paths and vantage points from which the city can be perceived.

For the first part of the visual survey, the city site is classified into six basic ground forms:

- Level, gently sloping or rolling sites
- Sloping sites, backed by hills or steeper slopes
- Valley or gorge sites
- Amphitheatrical or fan-shaped sites
- Bowl-shaped sites
- Ridged or hill top sites

The manmade features are classified into five forms:

- Urban textures
- Green areas
- Circulation facilities
- Paved open spaces
- Individually significant architectural masses, including vertical and horizontal forms.

For the second part of the visual survey, Williams has developed five ways through which the city may be perceived and experienced: the panorama, the skyline, the vista, urban open space, and through the experience of the individual in motion.

The manmade environment of the Delhi is a physical expression of the social, economic and technological conditions of our age. It mirrors society at a given period of time. Delhi's buildings can be no greater than the sense of responsibility and patronage from which they originate. The Metropolis reflects people and renders their achievements quantifiable.

In many arenas of Delhi, politics, private interests, commercial greed and urban planning and architecture clash. The results show up clearly in the profiles, skylines and silhouettes of the Metropolis. They show up in its many genres of urban planning and urban design, ranging from the erroneous and grandiose, to the organic and humble. In brief, Delhi is indeed the true image of people, depicting their fortes and failures.

In all great historic periods, be they Ancient, Mediaeval, Renaissance or Contemporary, socio-economic conditions expressed themselves in the physical structure of cities. The cities, then, had a character of their own, which lent to their imagability.

The old cities of India, for instance, whether resulting from planning or organic growth, reflected multiple level of organisations. There was an identifiable hierarchy of intricately linked functions, spaces and movement systems, from the scale of the city as a whole through that of the front door of the house.

In the walled cities, built by the Moghuls, Shahajahanabad, the main streets from the city gates, to its centre-defined identifiable quarters. Similar combinations of institutions within these districts, which were based on public services, markets or special functions, did establish local identity. The built form of Delhi Metropolis, with the exception of Lutyen's New Delhi, as we perceive it, can be characterized as an amorphous mass of sordidness, punctuated with patches of pompous and vulgar hideousness in the garb of so-called modern architecture.

Visually as well as functionally, much of the manmade townscape of Delhi appears so chaotic, as to defy any comprehension, and most of it contains such incessant repetition to the extent of being monotonous.

The fact that so much of the built form of Delhi is unimaginative and of poor quality is a reflection of a generally poor level of understanding and appreciation in our urban society, of the importance of architecture and urban design in the city-building process.

Delhi has been expanding haphazardly. The phenomenon of growing into amorphous mass of structures has been the dominant feature of urban expansion. The built form of Delhi is engendered by the initiative and enterprise of developers and builders acting individually and collectively. This community action needs to be guided through urban design expressing the basic principles and design guidelines, which should help shape the urban form of the city. The shape, design and character of Delhi are being strongly influenced by the so-called international style architecture. The materials and techniques used in the buildings are often motivated by expediency and economy with the result traditional culture, expressing a social and economic structure, and visual sensibility of a pervasive and unified tradition, is being gradually eroded by modern technology and convenience.

Prince Charles in the 'Vision of Britain' writes: "We do not have to live in surroundings which directly reflect the technology. Apart from anything else, such forms of design tend to ignore natural conditions, and are frequently energy inefficient, such as huge office blocks and the energy required to air-condition them, not to mention the effect on the ozone layer from the CFCs".

The residential architecture in Delhi's neighbourhoods reflects the disappearance of the regional styles and concepts. For instance, the house plan that looked outward on to the street. The cool and clean air and the serenity of the courtyard are replaced by the dust and noise of the street. Traditional house design which safeguarded against the severities of the climate is disregarded in favour of designs, which are ill-suited to the environment and rely heavily upon compensating mechanical aids.

Our own heritage of regional styles and individual characteristics has disappeared, replacing with hybrid, non-discript, and mediocre architecture. It is time we rediscovered the richness of our architectural past as well as the basic principles which made our old cities develop as they did.

Shouldn't we seek inspiration from the richness of our heritage? Dr. Hassan Fathy, the famous Egyptian architect said: "Because of the desire to abandon the past as an irrelevance, so much of priceless value has been lost or destroyed. The revealed knowledge of the sage is now replaced by so-called modernism, while the skill of the craftsman's hand has been replaced by the machine". Tradition need not rule out progress.

It was Edmund Burke who wrote: "A healthy civilization exists with three relationships intact: it has a relationship with the present, a relationship with the future and a relationship with the past. When the past feeds and sustains the present and the future, you have a civilized society".

We have broken that fact with the past and tried to obliterate its meanings and its messages. Today, unfortunately the pervasive pattern of planned development is to alter beyond recognition, the existing environment, rather than acknowledge the value of what exists and weave into it the desired new.

The increasing use of motor vehicles is also responsible for altering the face of Delhi; this is so, not only in India but the world over. We habitually sacrifice all the special values of the city to the function of motorized transportation.

The car-oriented, anti-city projects such as elevated urban highways and flyovers have intruded upon, if not destroyed sections of Delhi wiping out streets and urbanism in their wake.

Peter Wolf in "The Future of the City" writes: "To redesign cities to accommodate the car is to redesign cities out of existence. The car and the city are natural enemies. To experience the city one must be able to participate in it, to walk the streets, take a public transit. The inherent anti-urban qualities of the car are still not generally recognized".

For instance, Europeans build cars to fit the city. Over here, we are building the city to fit the car. While motorized transportation is critical for Delhi, it is too important to be looked upon only as a method of moving people, goods and services. Transportation must be seen as a means of designing a more satisfactory urban environment; for much that would be done to improve the environment, would also help improve transportation. In fact this two-way relationship between transportation and the city structure and form could prove to be the key to urban revolution in India. It is essential, therefore, that we develop principles and techniques to link effectively the handling of motor traffic with the designing or restructuring our cities. As early as 1973, the union government seized with the imminent danger to the aesthetic of the National Capital introduced legislative measures to regulate the quality of the built form, by enacting 'Delhi Urban Art Commission' Act 1973 that established the Art Commission.

The Commission's role was of advising union government in the matter of preserving, developing and maintaining aesthetic quality of urban and environmental design of the Metropolis of Delhi; and of advising and guiding local authorities in respect of any project of building and engineering operation or any development proposal which affects the aesthetic quality of the surroundings or any public amenity provided therein.

It is unfortunate that even after four decades the aesthetic quality of Delhi's built form leaves much to be desired.

Chapter 8
Metropolitan transportation

The road pattern of Delhi was fixed well before the advent of motor age. So long as transportation was mostly by public transport and bicycles, there was no traffic congestion. Today, Delhi Metropolis is threatened with the onslaught of millions of cars and motorcycles/scooters plying on roads with inadequate capacity and with intersections at frequent intervals, each of which is potential obstruction to the smooth traffic flow, leading to endless traffic gridlocks.

Traffic congestion makes it hard to get around the Metropolis. Too many cars have turned roads into parking lots. A motor vehicle wastes on an average 1.6 litres of fuel in traffic jams, amounting to total wastage of 3 million litres of fuel. Cars, motorcycles/scooters idling at 600 traffic signals burn Rs. 1000 crore worth of fuel per year. Traffic gridlocks consume 90 minutes of commuter time. Loss of man hours and productivity runs into billions of rupees.

Cars and motorcycles, scooters and other motor vehicles are a major source of nitrogen oxide and volatile organic compounds, which interact to form ground-level ozone and microscopic particulate matter that is key component of air pollution.

Letting unlimited use of cars and motorcycles, without solving resulting congestion by controlling the use by providing alternatives, has led to deterioration of Delhi's transportation and its livability. The growth of cars and motorcycles has been so prodigious that it is strangulating it own mobility. Today there are over 7 million motor vehicles in the Metropolis. The rising tide of these vehicles, with over 3 million added every year, will not put a stop to itself, until it has almost put a stop to the traffic. For the car-centric Delhi, approaching gridlock, to the extent of being paralysed, a better solution is needed.

First of all, car use has to be restricted as a measure for reducing congestion in a constrained urban space in the Metropolis. Those driving private cars do not bear costs commensurate with the increment of costs their use imposes. People using private cars consider the costs to themselves of the time, petrol and car depreciation; but do not take into account the costs, loss of time they impose on every other driver. Nor do they consider the traffic congestion they all contribute to.

This makes it necessary to levy charge on drivers of private cars for the full cost of their commute, in terms of a fee for the impact their cars impose on rest of the road. Charging cars for extra cost incurred by the Metropolis of Delhi to provide car drivers with road capacity, during rush hours, is one way to bring about a more equitable use of road space.

For road-pricing policy to be efficacious, a marked improvement in all modes of public transit is imperative. It will have to be an attractive alternative to travel by an individual mode. The Government of the National Capital Territory of Delhi instead has been subsidizing the car users, by providing flyovers at exorbitant costs, when 70 per cent of the citizens do not own cars.

Delhi Metropolis can only be made to function efficiently and provide a decent environment for living, is by giving a new dynamic role to mass transit on which majority of the citizens depend on. Unless, mass transit has precedence over individual mode of travel, parts of the Metropolis that are already destroyed, to make way for the proliferating car and motorcycle traffic, will be further pulled down, in an attempt to get rid of traffic congestion, only to find that congestion still remains; while the aesthetic character of the historic and social value, neither of which, should be compromised to provide unlimited travel by car and motorcycle. Let us not mortgage the future of our nation's capital for the expediencies of the present.

There are two fundamental issues in urban planning: environment and transportation. Environment has precedence over transportation because the ultimate goal of urban planning is to improve living conditions. Therefore, transportation should be the means of designing a more satisfying urban environment, in the process urban mobility would well be served.

The two-way relationship between transportation and urban environment underscores the need to device means of transportation to fit the Metropolis of Delhi, instead of forcing its fabric to fit the traffic. Europeans build cars to fit the city. We here in Delhi are building our city to fit the car. Peter Wolf in his book "The Future of the City" writes: "To redesign cities to accommodate the car, is to redesign cities out of existence".

To be considered efficient, mass transportation system must be available to all parts of Delhi Metropolis. It must be accessible to all sections of population and must provide easy access to work places, central business areas, train stations, airports, health and education centres, markets and shopping centres, and the like. It must satisfy travel volume requirements, satisfy performance (speed, safety, reliability and comfort), reasonable fare, provide facilities and services, that are efficiently incorporated with a human-oriented urban environment, and stimulate creation of desirable urban development form.

No single mode of transport can ever satisfy the diverse needs of the Delhiites. Travel choices are made based on individual needs, which vary substantially by location, time and distance and category of the traveller. The diverse needs are met by walking, cycling, car, motorcycle, DTC bus service, Delhi Metro Rail, suburban trains, auto rickshaw and taxis. Each type of transport has its special use, and a good transportation policy must seek to improve each type and create an integrated multimodal transportation system.

To coordinate the individual choices into an efficient multimodal transportation system, it is necessary to draw up a comprehensive plan to utilize the benefits of diversity. Each mode must be planned separately and then integrated with other modes, through an iterative planning and design process. Such coordination must be both at the planning of infrastructure and at the operational level. The greatest advantage of putting in place an integrated multimodal system of transport is that it would result in economically efficient, socially integrated and environmentally livable Metropolis of Delhi.

No other phase of urban services is handled by so many different agencies of Delhi state government, as traffic and transportation, and no other phase receives as little attention in scientific and traffic engineering planning. In order to deal efficaciously and comprehensively with the nature of traffic and transportation problems, it is imperative to put in place a single command under a metropolitan transportation authority, to ensure planning, coordination, budgeting, programming and phasing of projects for modernising traffic operations, providing a multimodal integrated transportation system and for providing off-street parking facilities.

Walking and cycling as effective transportation mode

The oldest form of human transportation is walking. In Delhi, pedestrians are a very important factor. As many as 35 per cent of the total daily trips are walking: trips to work, shop or transact business. High-speed transport and quest for efficiency killed the once walkable Delhi. Each advance in transportation technology, from tongas and bicycles, to buses and cars and urban highways, has degraded the pedestrian environment in the National Capital. For pedestrian or bicyclist, it is impossible to move about freely. The street pattern in our residential areas is inhospitable to pedestrians and bicycles and lack sidewalks.

Planners have ignored the importance of pedestrian traffic to the quality of life, in the urban development process. Walking is crucial for livability, to which the Delhi Development Authority has not paid much attention, while neglecting urban planning and design at micro scale. Micro-design is urban design of individual areas in the Delhi Metropolis that often has a major influence on the roles of different modes of travel, particularly on pedestrians, especially in residential areas and places like Connaught Place, district centres, community centres, markets and shopping centres, making them more walkable and for people to meet.

Most cities in Europe, in order to enhance social life and livability, encourage pedestrian activities in their central business districts, as well as in the shopping centres. In Delhi, where a large number of people walk, they remain marginalised. In our entrancement with the car, we have forgotten how much more efficient and how much more flexible the foot-walker is.

Roads in Delhi are inhospitable to pedestrians and lack sidewalks. The entire system has been designed for the convenience of the motorists. At present, it is virtually impossible for people walking to navigate freely in the city, thereby, imperiling their safety. In the fatality toll, pedestrians outnumber drivers of motor vehicles. People walking in Delhi have generally been subjected to relatively little control and provided for very inadequately. There is a great need to construct facilities that would make it easier for people to walk safely and conveniently.

In the United States, a major shift in policy, away from auto-centric planning to mandated accommodation of the pedestrian and bicycle in federally supported transportation projects, has stimulated numerous pedestrian and bicycle policies, plans, and built projects across the country. Our built environment must support and encourage walking, by providing comfort and safety for pedestrians, as well as offering visual interest in their journeys through Delhi. It must be made interesting enough socially to make one feel that walking is more than just getting from one place to another.

Walkability might be defined as the extent to which the built environment supports and encourages walking, by providing for pedestrian comfort and safety; connecting people with varied destinations, within a reasonable amount of time and effort; and offering visual interest in journeys throughout Delhi.

One fundamental principle must be maintained that pedestrians have precedence over all other road users. Pedestrians must be given priority over vehicular traffic in shopping centres, markets, business districts and other commercial areas that generate pedestrian traffic in large numbers.

Walking and cycling are essential ingredients in an integrated, inter-modal transportation system to give travellers transportation options and to provide continuity from home to destination, through convenient and accessible links to other modes such as DTC bus, Delhi Metro, and suburban train, within a reasonable time distance of 10–15 minutes' walk.

Next to walking is the use of bicycles. Bicycles have several attractions for the user. For one thing, he or she is not spending money on fares or fuel. The bicycles provide the user with excellent physical exercise, recommended by doctors for strengthening the healthy heart. Bicycles take up relatively little space, create no traffic jams, or pollute the air; a cyclist is unlikely to cause any damage to pedestrians. On the positive side, the cyclist has advantage over the car driver, being above the car and being unenclosed he or she has all round vision. The cyclist has a non-stop door-to-door journey, which the car driver spends some time looking for a parking place. He or she can ride through red lights and difficult intersections, and negotiate traffic jams. For the short trips, involving several stops for shopping and so on, the cyclist may take little longer than the car, but experience none of the car driver's frustrations.

During the preparation of the first Master Plan for Delhi, in the late 1950s, traffic survey enumerated around 0.7 million bicycles in Delhi, which then had a population of less than 2 million people. The cyclists were seen riding on the streets for want of separate bicycle tracks.

To cater to such a large volume of bicycles, the Delhi Master Plan 1981 proposed express bicycle tracks, separated from motorized traffic, indicating the alignment of the tracks on the land-use plan. Like many others, this proposal too never got on the ground.

Figure 8.1 Delhi witnesses some of the worst urban ills due to haphazard and tremendous growth of the city. Traffic snarls are everyday occurrences in the crowded ITO area of the city.

In Delhi, both the state and the local governments have forgotten or ignored this relatively low-tech mobility option. It is about time to improve bicycle facilities and enhance safety, by creating city-wide bicycle network of express tracks.

A number of European cities have taken steps to substantially limit automobile traffic in their central areas. Some cities have converted their centres to car-free districts, limited to bicycles and pedestrians and public transport. There exists a network known as "Car-Free Cities" based in Brussels, of about 60 cities, working on these issues. Many of these participating cities are signatories to Copenhagen Declaration, making a commitment to finding ways to reduce the pressure of cars in their cities. Here in Delhi, we have produced an urban design for Delhi, so hostile to pedestrians and cyclists, to accommodate the car.

Parking crisis

After battling through traffic jams, finding a parking space is even more frustrating. There is scarcely a business and shopping areas in Delhi that is not handicapped by a lack of an adequate amount of parking facilities. And yet, neither the state nor the local government in Delhi has found a single, simple solution for the parking problem, with the result motor vehicles are parked on the road-kerbs, thereby reducing the traffic-carrying capacity of the road, to as much as 50 per cent.

Delhi's parking woes is now global news. Of the 20 big cities surveyed across the world, Delhi was rated the worst in terms of parking pain. The "Parking Index" formulated by IBM is based on peoples' response to the time taken for finding a parking space, not finding it, disagreement over parking space, and getting 'Challan' for illegal parking.

Delhi with a global parking index of 140 tops the list of 20 world cities. Inefficient parking system is a major setback to Delhi's productivity, leading to inefficient services. The frustration and pain of looking for parking space has impacted on the social behaviour of car drivers. Fights over parking have become all too common in the capital. With 7 million vehicles and 1000 more being added every day, parking space is woefully limited.

With the dire need for parking facilities, so apparent in this vast Metropolis, it seems incongruous that plans for road and highway improvements for moving motor vehicles are taking shape, while little or nothing is done for their parking. Certainly, roads and highways cannot be effective without adequate parking provisions, for motor vehicles they carry. Parking provisions must be integrated with facilities for movement of vehicles. Mere movement does not accomplish the ends of transportation. Motor vehicles have no utility to their owners, unless it is possible to park the vehicles, once the driver has reached his destination.

Figure 8.2 Even in a place like Connaught Place, which was well planned, design has gone for a toss as burgeoning buildings, each accommodating hundreds of people, have thrown all traffic out of gear.

Every car in Delhi occupies large amount of space, for its movement and storage. It needs a parking space at home, a parking space at place of destination, like employment, business, shopping, and of course a space on the road for movement. It won't occupy all the three or more spaces at once, but nevertheless spaces have to be there.

Parking requirements for different purposes necessitate different types and operation of facilities. For instance, worker parking is generally all-day parking and must be available at low rates, usually on self-parking basis. Shoppers, usually are short-term parkers, need to be charged on hourly basis. Those wishing to transact business often park for only a few minutes at a time, but often many times a day, can be accommodated at the kerb with parking meters.

Local government in Delhi can provide for these different needs by careful selection and development of appropriate sites, and application of rate schedules to encourage desired usage. Kerb spaces reserved for short-term parking to be enforced by parking meters, which wherever in use, have proved their value in the effective control of time-limit parking along the kerb. They result in a greater parking turnover and tend to eliminate the all day parker.

The eventual step is to prohibit parking in congested areas of Connaught Place, Chandni Chowk, and other congested business districts, for a time longer than necessary. But this can only be achieved after adequate off-street parking is provided. However, the space available for off-street parking is limited to cater to increasing demand for parking, in already congested business centres.

The pressure on available parking spaces can be relieved to the extent that commuters to congested business and commercial areas are persuaded to use mass transportation, rather than private mode of travel.

The Municipal Corporation of Delhi has not made much progress in providing off-street car parks. Between 2003 and 2007, the MCD announced building of 40 car parks. In 2003, MCD announced construction of 16 automated multilevel car parks; and in late 2007, 24 conventional car parks.

When parking has assumed crisis proportions, the MCD needs to speed up the construction of the car parks announced by it, and at the same time not permit high-density redevelopment in Delhi, without providing corresponding street capacity and off-street parking.

Regional transport linkages

The solution to Delhi's transportation problems does not lie just in the National Capital Territory of Delhi along, but also it very much depends on the linkages to the towns in Delhi Metropolitan area, as well as in the towns in the NCR.

A large number of vehicles come to Delhi and leave the Metropolis during peak hours; the highest traffic volume being on National Highway 24 (Delhi–Ghaziabad), followed by NH-8 (Delhi–Gurgaon). The road from Faridabad NH-2 is equally chocked. This traffic is generated because of jobs and businesses in the capital.

There is a suburban train service operating between Delhi and towns in NCR for quite some time. It is grossly inadequate, unreliable and inconvenient, because of lack of feeder service from trip-end points.

Due to development of towns in NCR, there is an urgent need to strengthen available rail service capacity along the tracks, and provide dedicated electrified corridors, automatic signaling facilities, additional suburban stations, rolling stock and power supply; and integrate the suburban rail system with the Ring Railway and the Delhi Metro. The Ring Railway carries less than 1 per cent of the commuter load. The main hurdle is limited capacity in the northern stretch of the Ring, inadequate feeder service, and lack of integration with radial railway lines. There isn't any scope for improving capacity in the northern stretch – between Tilak Bridge and New Delhi Station, but it is possible to augment capacity in the Southern Stretch. The NCR Planning Board has recommended suburban railway development projects to provide fast mass transit connectivity to the Ring towns – Ghaziabad, Meerut and Bulandshahr in UP; Sonepat, Gurgaon, Faridabad and Rohtak in Haryana; and Alwar in Rajasthan – identified as major contributors to Delhi's increasing migrant population. The mass transit connectivity will also serve as a catalyst for the development of these Ring towns within NCR, fostering their growth. Promoting regional growth is a way to relieve population congestion in Delhi, enabling middle and working class families to move to better homes in less-crowded neighbourhoods.

The suburban rail system has a capacity to carry about 0.04–0.06 million people per hour along a single route; whereas, highways using more space cannot move more than 0.004–0.006 million cars with an average occupancy of more than 1.5 passengers. The NCR is home to nearly 40 million people. In recent years, significant social and economic changes have occurred in the region. These changes have created demand for travel that the present transportation system must meet.

The NCR is at the centre of railway network for passenger and freight traffic. There are five radial railway lines and the ring railway, which are significantly tied to NCR's transportation requirements, both intra and interstate. The NCR is also at the centre of national highway network. There are five radial national highways and the concentric ring roads.

To cope up with the travel demand, there is a proposal for creating two orbital railway corridors. The outer corridor will have a length of 300 km and will connect Panipat, Rohtak, Rewari, Palwal, Khurja, Hapur and Meerut.

The inner corridor will connect Sonepat, Sampla, Jhajjhar, Gurgaon, Faridabad and Dadri. There is also a proposal for separate expressways to connect Panipat, Rewari, Rohtak, Palwal, Meerut and Bhagpath and for Ghaziabad—Hapur link: the Western Peripheral Expressway (Kundli, Manesar–Palwal); Taj Expressway (Greater Noida–Balia); the Eastern Peripheral Expressway (Kundli-Ghaziabad–Palwal).

Since Delhi is linked to Noida and Gurgaon with Delhi Metro, many car drivers travelling between Noida and Delhi and Gurgaon and Delhi have switched on to Delhi Metro, on Park-and-Ride basis. For those travellers, where Metro stations are not within walking distance, efficient DTC bus feeder service is imperative.

The Union Urban Development Ministry has approved in principle a rail-based regional rapid transit system to provide fast connectivity between Delhi and Meerut, Alwar, and Panipat. Conceived as multi-modal system, integrated with Delhi Metro,

DTC bus cluster and terminals will not only ease connectivity to distant towns in NCR, but also will ease traffic congestion on roads.

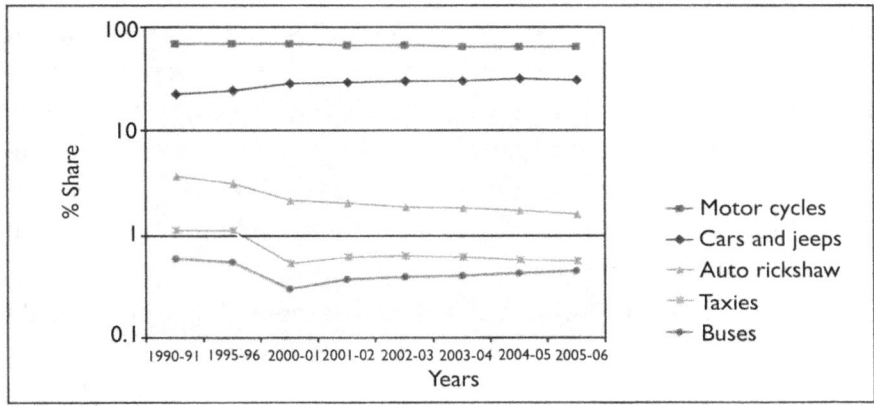

Source: Drawn from data available by transport department, government of NCT of Delhi

Figure 8.3 Types of motor vehicles in Delhi as percentage (%) share

These three corridors, Delhi–Ghaziabad–Meerut, Delhi–Gurgaon–Alwar, and Delhi–Sonepat–Panipat, need to be executed sooner than 25 years, as stipulated by the authorities. It brooks no delay, because the population of NCR is rising at an exponential rate. It shot up 40% to 21.7 million people in the last decade.

A good transportation system supports social, economic and environmental well-being of the people in the region. The way we deal today with the issues of land development, accessibility, economic vitality, mobility and environmental protection, will affect the quality of life for years to come.

The provision of good transportation service is expensive and financial resources are limited. It is important, therefore, to plan future major transportation for NCR to ensure the best system possible, with the financial resources expected to be available.

The US government enacted Intermodal Surface Transportation Efficiency Act in 1991. The Act requires state and regional authorities to plan comprehensively appropriate modes of transportation. It calls for a holistic approach to transportation planning by considering a range of transportation modes, their impact on natural and built environment.

The NCR planning board, instead of a piece meal approach to addressing regional transportation planning, should formulate a comprehensive regional transportation plan for providing an integrated and coordinated multimodal transportation system; a system that maintains accessibility and includes a variety of mobility options, which serve the needs of residents and business in the NCR. With significant support to all modes of travel, such as, bus, Delhi Metro, suburban rail, cars, motorcycles will improve regional mobility and accessibility.

The regional transportation plan will be a long-range guide for major investments in NCR's multimodal transportation system. Agencies such as Delhi Transport Corporation, Delhi Metro, Northern Railways and the Public Works Department responsible for operating and maintaining the transport system will have to develop their own plans and programmes within the framework of the regional transportation plan, which will recommend major projects, systems, policies and strategies designed to maintain existing infrastructure and meet future travel demands.

Changes in regional development have contributed to a rapid growth in suburban-to-suburban trips in NCR. At the same time, the demand for the suburbs to city trip has remained strong. This combination of travel pattern has added a new dimension to the challenge of serving regional travel needs.

In addition to a shift in travel pattern, the individual choice of mode in NCR has continued to change. The role of car has grown dramatically. A sound transportation system must respond to significant changes in NCR, including commuting pattern and residential development.

Adjustments or changes to regional transportation system are to be made through a well-defined planning process. Transportation by its very nature is multi-jurisdictional and its issues need to be discussed at a regional level. The NCR planning board needs to establish a planning process that involves local, state and central governments in the formulation of the regional transportation plan.

Given the size and the complexity of NCR, the regional transportation plan cannot adequately address the many local issues and concerns that affect specific towns throughout NCR. The regional planning process must recognize the impact of regional travel pattern and transport improvements in these small areas.

The planning process must involve the states of Haryana, Uttar Pradesh and Rajasthan, as well as the local elected and appointed officials, professional staff from many unites of local governments, regional and local transport providers such as, railways, Delhi Metro, DTC; planners and residents – representatives of business.

Chapter 9
Vision for Delhi

Urban planning in operation in Delhi since the mid-1950s has focussed on land-use planning and development control, and not on a vision of what Delhi, the National Capital, should be. The key ingredient in helping to bring about a successful city is forging a vision of what Delhi can be; an inspiring yet realistic vision that incorporates development and change as well as the protection of natural and cultural resources and character.

Successful cities incorporate many elements – commercial vitality, jobs, good educational institutions, health care, a mix of housing types, adequate mass public transportation system, efficient delivery of urban services – water and electricity, that go beyond environmental and aesthetic concerns.

Nevertheless, how a city looks and feels, how it treats its heritage, says much about whether there is in fact a sense of community, a sense of caring by its residents about its future. Our vision for Delhi, as the national capital, should entail both protecting its distinctive assets and creating quality development that builds on and enhances such resources.

The historic monuments, architectural heritage, the Ridge, the Yamuna River, parks and open spaces are the natural and cultural assets that make Delhi distinctive. Delhi's assets and distinctive character are what inspire people, create a sense of concern and motivate action. We will not get very far in developing a vision for the future without focusing our efforts on the positive assets Delhi has or can create.

Delhi is dominated by mundane buildings of little interest. With the exception of few parts, everywhere one sees the unsightliness of the manmade urban environment – a wanton destruction through development. Construction of buildings is guided only by the anarchy of individual enterprise and builders in search of quick profits. Delhi – the national capital – has degenerated into a city without a soul, a conglomeration of suburbs, most of them non-descript.

Delhi once had a special quality about it, but which has since become just another unrecognizable part of a larger, amorphous, sprawling metropolitan area. The enormous pressure of massive urban growth and development and consequential effects on the urban landscape are overwhelming. We urgently need to find effective strategies that will enable the Metropolis of Delhi to develop in ways that enhance, not degrade, the qualities that lend it distinction and character. What makes a city successful rests largely in the eye of the beholders. It is more a subjective judgement and a feeling, than quantifiable factors and data. Let us then ask ourselves – Is Delhi a good place, to live, to work, to raise a family, to enjoy leisure time? These are commonly the needs fulfilled by cities considered successful.

Historic–cultural preservation

Delhi has significant historical and cultural resources that, properly protected, can significantly enhance its livability and distinctiveness. Lack of public appreciation of the value of preserving local historic and cultural resources contributes to the threat of demolition and degradation of these resources. The plan for Delhi should document the numerous values, to the people of Delhi, of its historic and cultural resources, and articulate priority for preserving these resources. We should have a cultural policy that must be concerned with the preservation and transmission of the best of our heritage works that have been ratified by the test of time.

River Yamuna: Protecting and enhancing it

Historically, rivers have been the birthplace of world's great civilizations. Delhi was born on the banks of the river Yamuna. The river Yamuna is the birthplace of Delhi and serves as a principal source of water supply for the National Capital. Given the central importance of the Yamuna to local development, it is a key asset and provides a good focus around which to build local conservation and growth management efforts. Protecting Yamuna and the lands adjacent to it serves multiple public objectives, namely: protecting people and property from flood damages; protecting quantity and quality of water for public drinking supply; protecting fish and wildlife habitat; and promoting scenic and recreational values.

The rapid growth of unauthorised colonies, discharging sewage into the river is the problem. The Delhi Jal Board finds it tough to provide sewerage in such densely populated colonies, where there is barely road space for undertaking the work. There is also a massive encroachment on the banks of the river, causing contamination. With the quality of Yamuna water deteriorating at alarming extent, drastic measures brook no delay. Loss of public access due to inappropriate river front development; impervious urban surfaces that increase runoff and flood hazards during rainy season; increased turbidity and sedimentation due to soil erosion. We need a local river protection programme, for water is a basic necessity of life for the Delhiites. Clean water supply is critical to public environmental health. A comprehensive programme must be drawn up to protect and enhance Yamuna River resources. Focus attention on protecting an entire watershed.

At the time of writing this book, a river front development project was on the anvil that aimed to conserve, protect and restore the biodiversity of the river, integrating with public recreation. The project highlights creation of recreational spaces on both banks; revival of river's flora and fauna; and of developing green spaces. The bio-community once found on river bed has depleted due to pollution, necessitating development of biodiversity zone.

Urban design

The chaos and waste with which Delhi has expanded poses a challenge to our concept of health, happiness and welfare. Such an urban form has destroyed our very perception of home and family. Delhi's urban form derives from simply the addition of undifferentiated parts without any philosophical guiding principles.

The suburban residential areas, irrespective of income levels of the residents, have no identity or a sense of place. The Delhi Metropolis has grown guided only by the anarchy of individual enterprise and builders.

In order to obviate the vastness and lack of differentiation in the 'megalopolis' into which the nation's capital finds itself, a clearly definable unit of urban life will have to be deviced, which might serve as a cell of a restructured Delhi. We need counter movement, directed against metropolitan congestion and the urban sprawl. The relief of congestion is not a matter of widening or expanding the suburban areas, but decentralising all its functions and urban development in relatively self-contained urban units, responsive to direct human contact and enjoying both urban and rural advantages/benefits.

The formation of the early city was due in the beginning, to man's ability to walk over a certain area within a reasonable period of time. This led to a city which can be enclosed within a square of 2000 yards. When increasing numbers of people could no longer be accommodated within the small city of the past, growth led to the metropolis. However, the metropolis could not operate properly until it was organised into a system of small cities or townships.

Unfortunately, Delhi Metropolis does not have a structure serving its increasing complexity, in the same way as the structure of the past served the complexity existing in those days.

It is neither the size nor rate of growth of Delhi Metropolis alone is the cause of the urban problem, instead it is the lack of proper structure for the national capital. Delhi Metropolis cannot operate properly, unless it is organized into a system of small townships. We need to divide the metropolis into physical units of optimum size, which will lay the foundation for the organisation of future Delhi.

Growing experience in municipal administration has pointed out the need, not only for more coordination over a broader area of the National Capital, but also for a greater degree of decentralisation in the decisions and programmes which directly affect the everyday lives of Delhiites.

Cities-within-cities concept of urban design could provide answer to restoring Delhi Metropolis to the human scale by breaking down of the vast spread out metropolis into social units.

Jorge Arango in his book "The Urbanisation of the Earth" suggests a system of self-contained urban units, integrated with open land, making possible and practical the control of city growth in both quantity and quality. His urban unit is a sector of approximately 2 square miles, of homogeneous character (Two square miles means a 15-minute walk from the farthest point to the centre). The urban units are separated from one another by green channels, the interurban landscape, open land from 1800 feet to one half mile wide, where the main lines of transportation, communications, and services are inconspicuously laid.

James Howard Kunstler in his book 'Home from Nowhere' talks about creating an alternative model of the human habitat for the 21st century – a model of the everyday environment. The model is structured on the principle of the basic unit of planning, being the residential neighbourhood. A cluster of neighbourhoods becomes a bigger town. Clusters of a great many neighbourhoods become a city. The population of a neighbourhood can vary, depending on local conditions. The neighbourhood is limited in physical size, which is defined as a 5-minute walking distance or a quarter-mile radius. Human scale is the standard for proportion in buildings and their accessories. Cars and other vehicles are permitted, but do not take precedence over human needs, including aesthetic needs. The neighbourhood contains a public-transit stop.

Cities do not deteriorate overnight and similarly are not reborn overnight. Urban planners need to test the possibility of creating a viable urban form for a nation's capital, by building an experimental model that would set a new pattern for future development. This is essential, because the formless growth of Delhi is neither economical nor satisfactory. To plan for an alternative to the amorphous mass of urban sprawl that metropolitan Delhi has become – we must radically revive our concept of urban planning. The planners must change constant urban expansion of piecemeal addition to orderly decentralisation in self-contained "townships" to halt the continued congestion and expansion of the capital which is spilling over into Haryana and Uttar Pradesh. There is a need to evolve a concept to guide the transformation of our suffocating national capital.

We need to develop a prototype of urban form for Delhi. Planners of today must have imaginative and courageous views our changing times require. We have to accept the inevitability of Delhi Metropolis, of a size, not previously seen in world history. In this context, the problems of the immediate future would cluster around finding an efficient metropolitan design, one that would solve the social and physical problems of 'Delhi Megapolis'. Planned megapolises, Richard Meier argues, would be far preferable to the haphazard growth of urban conurbation. Meier's solution to the design problem is the Cellular Megapolis, each cell taking the form of an 'urban village'.

System must be adaptable to existing urban pattern of Delhi so that it can be applied without interference to its normal functioning, and in the amount and at the speed proportionate to Delhi's needs and means. The benefits should be felt from the beginning even when started in a modest and limited way. It is not a plan per se, rather it is a way in which city should be organised so that it can be planned. It is a strategy for giving the city a more developed organisation.

There is an urgent need to take a hard look at how we create physical environments. It calls for a more dynamic, more inclusive design process. What would make Delhi a better place than it is at present? How do we know and who gets to decide? Technology-oriented investments of the future will go to those cities in India that can attract the nation's college-educated workforce, which puts a premium on cities perceived as good places to live and work. While current trends will influence the future, it is the very place of change, technological innovations, and economic transformation that are likely to shape the next several decades of the new millennium, in ways that seem hard to imagine. We find ourselves living in an era of extraordinary transition, not just technological, but also psychological. Such times call for the new breed of political leadership in local government armed with a vision and agenda for taking Delhi Metropolis along new paths to meet the challenge. The city of the 19th Century in the west offered new technological wonders, job opportunities and a whole new value system, based on a seemingly limitless material prosperity. Financial panics, crowded housing, poverty and disease, and the destruction of traditional rural values of individualism and independence attended the growth of the city in an industrial age. But the prospects of money and the excitement of the new age proved to be the greater lure than the disadvantage proved to be repellents. Furthermore, as the 19th Century drew to a close, a generation of urban reformers looked at the city with opportunistic faith that all its ills could be cured.

Technology is reshaping city life in Delhi and making it more intellectually productive. Digital technology has begun to blanket the Metropolis, forming the backbone of a large infrastructure. Broadband, fibre optics and wireless telecom towers, so ubiquitous in Delhi's skyline, are supporting mobile phones, smart phones and tablets that are increasingly affordable. Similarly, open data can be downloaded from websites and add to, are revealing all kinds of information; and public cybercafés are helping literate and illiterate access it. Relentless growing network of sensors and digital control technologies, all tied together by cheap powerful computers, making the Delhi Metropolis look like 'Computers in Open Air'.

The vast amount of data emerging in the cyber space is perhaps the starting point for making efficient infrastructure programmable for optimising Delhi's daily process, the use of pervasive computing to optimise urban systems, from transportation to energy.

Getting information about actual road conditions can reduce traffic and improve air quality. In order to restrict the use of car, particularly during rush hours in central business areas of Delhi, road pricing policy can be implemented efficaciously by installing cameras that automatically identify licence plates of vehicles entering the business districts and charge drivers the entry fee per day, depending on where the vehicles go. The potential for developing more of this kind of efficient infrastructure is vast and a good fraction can be unleashed through 'smart systems'.

Many corporations like IBM, CISCO System, Siemens and more have been setting their sites on the urban space. An understanding of how cities actually develop, gives an opportunity to radically rethink what intelligent wired Delhi Metropolis of the future could look like and how it can be designed, built and lived in. Delhi will emerge as a smart city, as citizens and their many electronic devices are recruited as real-time sensors of daily life. Networking the ubiquitous sensors and linking them to government database can enhance Delhi's inventiveness, efficiency and services. With proper technical support structure, the citizens can tackle problems of energy use, traffic congestion and more.

How can we leverage digital technology to make Delhi Metropolis sustainable? However, Delhi will not be able to sustain itself, if left to function on a business-as-usual basis. Demands for resources will outstrip supply, as number of people swell from over 16 million to over 23 million by the year 2021.

As a centre of economic activity, Delhi Metropolis is a significant consumer of energy, and producer of greenhouse gases. It must not only conserve energy and limit carbon emission, but also diversify its energy supply. Ensuring sustainable supply of water to growing population of the capital is a daunting task for the Delhi Jal Board. Even for existing population, there is a wide gap between demand

and supply. The Board needs to launch water-efficiency programme, wherein it must offer incentives to curb water use, including rebate for installing rain water harvesting systems and water-conserving toilets.

The local government should encourage use of more energy-efficient and long-lasting building materials which could significantly enhance the sustainability of the Metropolis. This would necessitate changing building bye-laws to require more energy-efficient buildings. Local government must exploit creative solutions to reduce energy consumption, water use, waste and emissions, while also making it easier for people to get around.

There are places in the world that have demonstrated some creative solutions to reduce energy consumption and water use. In Berlin, photovoltaic sheets on south-facing building façade generate electricity. The Empire State Building in New York City has installed super insulated windows that quadruple the thermal performance of double panes.

In Rockville, Massachusetts, residential and commercial construction across the city is the highest green or leader in energy and environmental design standard, which saves energy and material. In Austin, Texas, water-saving toilets and showers installed in buildings save millions of litres of water annually. In San Francisco, California, digital parking meters inform mobile phone and navigation apps when a parking space opens up, reducing thereby traffic caused by drivers in search of parking space.

Concerns about the impact of energy consumption on Delhi's environment have not penetrated consciousness of the public nor of those who govern Delhi. In order to avoid catastrophic change and human hardship, Delhi government must examine energy consumption sector wise, such as transportation, industry, commercial and residential. Ultimately, government will have to rethink and convert fossil fuel economy to renewable sources. It would be wise to accumulate information regarding leading practices in the field of sustainable city development.

Epilogue

Ever since Delhi Development Authority embarked on planned development of Delhi, over four decades ago, there has been no review of the urban planning in operation, to evaluate its effectiveness. As a result, there have been no reforms to ensure there is no gap between contemporary urban planning theory and practice, on the one hand; and on the other hand, the capacity of the planning machinery in DDA to perform functions for which it was created.

Urban planners need to have knowledge of the process and causes of Delhi's urban growth, as well as of its economy. Although economic factors are responsible for Delhi's urban growth, they have not been given due importance in the planning process. What the DDA does or does not do to deal with the problems of urban expansion, change and deterioration has direct bearing on the stability of investments, on the ability to do business, and on the amenities of home and family life, for the millions of Delhi's citizens.

The powers must be realised that the problems the Metropolis of Delhi has been facing, cannot be resolved by adopting a static or complacent approach, but instead they have to strive with greater determination, than ever before, for planned development on a sustainable basis.

Some of the most critical urban problems that remain unresolved need to be addressed on a priority basis. If we neglect our Metropolis, we will be doing so to our peril.

(1) Rehabilitation

Nearly half of Delhi Metropolis's population of 16 million people live in about 2600 informal settlements of *jhuggi* clusters, urban villages and unauthorised colonies, in conditions that are a true insult to human dignity. These uncounted urban masses, despite the conditions in which they live, are an economic resource, contributing in large measure to the informal sector of Delhi's economy. Unfortunately, in our all-inclusive urban planning, resettling them is a colossal task. Instead retrofitting these settlements is the best way of cleaning urban living.

(2) Redensification

The core of the Delhi Metropolis, with Lutyen's bungalow area, and union government's employee housing in New Delhi Municipal Council area; and the defence services housing in the Delhi Cantonment, has low-rise houses. The core area of 87 km^2 with a population of 1.6 million people has a density of 4,900 persons per km2 compared to 9,300 persons per km^2 in the rest of the Metropolis. Lutyen's bungalow area resembles "Plantation Living", right in the heart of Delhi.

Non-redensification of the core area has led to urban sprawl. We should build 'up' rather than 'out'. Most of the residential buildings in the core area are from single storey to double storey. These low-rise structures need to be redeveloped to high rise with high population density. Number of storeys and population density should be determined on the basis of the holding capacity of the core area.

(3) Traffic and transportation management

Out of control proliferation of traffic is threatening to paralyse Delhi Metropolis. It is imperative to restrict car use, as a measure for reducing congestion, in a constrained urban space. Charging car drivers for extra cost incurred by the Metropolis, to provide car drivers with road capacity, during rush hours, is one way to bringing about a more equitable use of road space. Restricting car use will be effective only when local government provides an efficient and reliable mass transit system, as an alternative to car, as well as motorcycle.

It is imperative to put in place an integrated multimodal mass transit system, comprising the Delhi transit bus service, the Delhi Metro Rail and the suburban railway, as a unified metropolitan transit. Around 70 per cent of the daily trips are made on the three modes of mass transit. Therefore, government must fund mass transit, instead of subsidizing the car, the trips which amount to only 10 per cent of the total daily trips. Besides, 70 per cent of the citizens of the Metropolis do not own cars.

To improve traffic mobility on Delhi's road network, a traffic operation plan for improving road capacity and safety must be drawn up, as a basis for more effective traffic management.

(4) Environmental protection and sustainable development

In the absence of a well-defined policy on environmental protection and sustainable development, there is no evidence on increasing energy efficiency nor of reducing carbon emission in Delhi. As a centre of economic activity, the Delhi Metropolis is significant consumer of non-renewable energy. Delhi Metropolis needs to be sustainable so as to meet the needs of the present, without compromising the ability of future generation of citizens, to meet their own needs. The demands for limited resources will outstrip supply, as the number of people in the Metropolis swell to 23 million people by the year 2021.

Concerns about the impact of indiscriminate energy consumption on Delhi's environment have not penetrated consciousness of the citizens, nor of those who seem to be governing Delhi. To avoid any catastrophe or human hardship, it is imperative to frame a policy on environmentally safe and economically viable energy pathway, which will sustain human progress. Low-energy path is the best way towards sustainable development. Delhi must develop a practice of efficient energy use, and tap sources of renewable energy options, like solar, biomass and wind energy.

Index

13th Finance Commission, 35
74th Constitution Amendment 1992, 23
    12th Schedule, 23, 33
    policy making and execution, urban citizens' direct role, 34

A

Archaic planning model, 17
Architecture, 53

B

Bicycles, 72
Birla Committee 1951, 10
Brussels
    Car-Free Cities", 74

C

Capital budgeting function, 22
Car-free districts, 74
Cellular Megapolis, 87
Chronic housing shortage, 16
Cities-within-cities, 86
City-building strategy, 8
Civic services, 23
Cluster of neighbourhoods, 86
Colonies' regularization
    anti-planning phenomenon, 44
Colony coundries, 44
Community development movement, 54
Companionship of others, 48
Connaught Place Shopping Centre, 3–4

Conscious urban planning, 9
Cycling, 72

D

DDA (Delhi Development Authority), 14
   planners, 14–15
   as urban planning body, 22
Delhi, 1
   as a smart city, 89
   assets and distinctive character, 83
   built form, unimaginative and of poor quality, 64
   daily process, data emerging in the cyber space, 89
   economic conditions, 6–8
   environment, energy consumption impact, 90
   goods and services produced (GSDP), 6
   grass-root democracy, 33
   households, 7
   international style architecture, 64
   local governments, 32
   manmade townscape, incessant repetition to the extent of being monotonous, 64
   Master Plan, 10
   metropolitan administration, 34
   metropolitan government, 34
   municipal administration, growing experience, 86
   neighbourhoods' residential architecture, 64
   per capita income, 6–7
   planned areas, 7
   population density, 4
   population distribution, 4
   proposed technical support structure, 89
   sprawling metropolis, 16–17
   statutory boards, 32
   sustainable supply of water, 89–90
   transportation and its livability, 66–67
   urban design, 85–90
   urban planners, 12
   urban population, 9–10
   urban services, 34
Delhi Development Act 1957, 15
Delhi government
   regularization announced without clearance of layout plans, 44
Delhi Improvement Trust, 10
Delhi Jal board
   water-efficiency programme, 90

Delhi Master Plan 1981, 10
    bicycle tracks, 73
    limitations, 11
    important objectives, 12–13
Delhi Master Plan 2021, 15
Delhi master plans
    rigid land-use plans and development controls, 17
Delhi Megapolis'
    social and physical problems, 87
Delhi metropolis
    urban growth, 19
    complexity and dimensions of problems, 23
    urban government, managerial alternatives and its capacity, 34–35
    built form as amorphous mass of sordidness, 63
    human settlements, 38
    retrofitting, 28–31
    city core, reorganisation of, 29
        squatter settlements, 30
        strip-retail-trade, 30
        urban traffic, 30
Digital technology, 88
Delhi Urban Art Commission' Act 1973, 66
Diverse settlements, 1

E

Economic prosperity, 7
Elevated urban highways and flyovers
    car-oriented, anti-city projects, 65
Employment centres, scattering of, 28
Employment possibilities, 39
Existing residential neighbourhoods, 52
    redevelopment, 52–53

F

"Form of Cities, The"
    urban form, structure and quality, 62
Four-storeyed buildings, 52–53
"Future of the City, The"
    inherent anti-urban qualities of the car, 65–66

G

Global parking index, 74
Good housing management, 54
Good neighbourhood streets, 52
Good residential neighbourhood, 51
Good transportation service, 79

Government of National Capital Territory of Delhi, 6
control and direction powers, 32–33

H

Habitat Complex, 55
Heavily trafficked arterial roads, 30
High-rise residential buildings inaccessibility to the outdoors, 55
Historic-cultural preservation, 83–84
'Home from Nowhere' model of the everyday environment, 86
House
"catchment" area, 46
need for a physical environment, 46
neighbourhood size, 46–47
planning, proximity and convenience, 46
refugees, urban development projects, 10
Human scale, 86–87
Human-oriented urban environment, 69

I

Informal economy, 40
Informal gathering places, 47
Informal settlements, retrofitting of, 92

J

Job-seeking migrants, 18

K

Kerb spaces, 76

L

"Lal Dora" areas, 42–43
Land development
anarchic attitude, 44
Land subdivision, 25–26
regulation of, 56–57
residential area layout plan
developer's role, 58
planning authority's role, 57–58
preliminary subdivision plan approval, 58
Land subdivision regulation, 55–60, 56f, 57f
Land-use maps, 26
Land-use plan, 17, 24–26
local planning authorities, 26
monitoring, 26
societal changes, 26
Land-use planning, 28, 61
strategy, employment pattern, 28

Land-use regulations, 25
Land-use–transportation relationship, 27–28
  traffic characteristics, 27
  transportation models, 27
  urban pattern, 28
Lutyen's Delhi, 3f, 32
Lutyen's New Delhi, 3, 63
  planned residential areas, 44–45
  residential areas, 50
Lutyen's bungalow area Non-redensification, 92

M

Manmade environment, 62–63
Mass transit, 68–69
  connectivity, 77
Mass transportation system, 69
Master plan (s)
  5-year city development programme, 21–22
  critical urban issues, 16
  vexing problems, 16
Metropolis, 1
Metropolitan government
  monitoring mechanism, 35
  political, institutional and financial capacity, 35
Metropolitan transportation authority, 70
Motorized transportation, 65–66

Multimodal mass transit system, 93
Multimodal transportation system, 70
Municipal Corporation of Delhi off-street car parks, 76
Municipal corporations, 6
Mutual construction societies, 40

N

National Capital Region (NCR), 8
  Planning Board, 18
    comprehensive regional transportation plan, 80
    regional development plan, 19
    suburban railway development projects, 77
  regional planning process, 81
  suburban-to-suburban trips, 80
  multimodal transportation system, 80
Neighbourhood character, 52
Neighbourhood organisations, 48
Neighbourhood plan, 52
Neighbourhood streets, 47
Neotraditional development, 51
New Delhi Municipal Council, 32
"Ninth Delhi", 13

O

Off-street parking, 76
Orbital railway corridors, 78

P

Parking crisis, 74–76
Parking facilities, 74–75
"Parking Index", 74
Parking provisions, 75
Parking requirements, 75
Parking space, 74
Peak hours, 77
Pedestrian traffic, 71
Pedestrian-friendly neighbourhood, 47
Pedestrians, 71
Plan sanctioning, 21
Planned megapolises, 87
Planned residential areas, 16, 44–49, 46f
    post-independence plotted residential development, 45
Planning expertise, 21
Poor
    urban economy, government's possible role, 40
Post-independence suburban development, 53
Poverty
poor shelter, 39
Public housing, 41
Public open spaces, 49
Public servants, 34

Q

Quality of life, environmental factors, 50

R

Radical urban renewal, 29
Rail service capacity, 77
Rail-based regional rapid transit system, 78–79
Rapid urbanization, 9, 10
    visible and dehumanising manifestation, 38
Redesigned urban pattern, 31
Regional transport linkages, 76–81
Relatively affluent middle class, 7
Residential area
    as physical and social entity, 46
Residential enclaves without civic amenities, 50
Residential neighbourhood planning guidelines, 58–59
    bringing needs of daily living within walking distance, 59
    centrally located community facilities, 59
    open spaces and parks, Functional planning, 60
    parking facilities for residents, 59

pedestrian lanes or paths, 59–60
security through neighbourliness, 59
street network, 58–59
community facilities, 59
vegetation, skillful treatment, 60
Residential neighbourhoods, 46–49
Residential subdivision, 56
Residential welfare associations (RWAs), 54
Revitalising neighbourhoods, 50–55
Ring Railway, 77
River Yamuna, 84–85
  encroachment on the banks, 84
  loss of public access, 84
  river front development project, 84–85
Road-pricing policy, 68, 89
Rural migrant, 41

S

Sanctioning authorities, 48
Self-contained "townships", decentralization, 87
Self-managed neighbourhoods, 54
Shahjahanabad (Delhi) of the Moghul period, 2f

Shanty dwellers, 40
  entrepreneurial energy, 42
  local government and squatter communities, co-ordination of, 40–41
Shanty towns, 38–42
Short-term parkers, 76
Sidewalks, 71
Society of neighbourhoods, 54
Sprawling post-independence suburbs, 48
Sprawling suburban landscape, 47
Sqautters
  granting of land tenure, 41
  municipal governments' inability, 39
  self-help and mutual aid, government policy needed, 41–42
Squatter communities, 40
Squatter settlements, 4–5
Squatting, 39
  no policy either by Delhi government or local government, 39
  public lands, 39
Street markets, 40
Streetscapes, 48
Suburban rail system, 78
Suburban train service, 77
Sustainable city development, 90

T

Town planning, 9
  scheme, 9, 31
Traditional house design, 64–65
Traditional residential neighbourhoods
  sense of belonging, 53
Traffic congestion, 16, 30, 59, 67–69, 79, 89
Traffic hazards
  markets and shopping centres, 30
Traffic snarls, 73f
Transportation and urban environment, 69
Travel choices, 69–70
Trees planting, 50–51

U

Unauthorized colonies, 43–44
  issuing provisional regularization certificates, 44
    sub-standard residential areas, 43
    regularization of, 44
Uncounted urban masses, 92
Unskilled migrants, 7
Urban aesthetics, 61
  cities, aesthetic characteristics, 62

"Urban Aesthetics"
  visual survey' techniques, 62–63
Urban agglomeration, 8
Urban areas
  shanty townization, 42
Urban development, regional approach, 18–19
Urban development policies, 23
  action area plan, 24
  directive plan, 24
  national '5-year plans', 24
Urban expansion, 64
Urban form, 85
Urban governance, 33
Urban housing, 19
Urban land use, 24–25
Urban planners, 87
Urban planning, 9
  as local government administrative function, 36–37
  evaluating city's problems, 36
  field, 20–21
  no review to evaluate its effectiveness, 17
  objective, 20
  organization, 22
  Planners' role, 36–37
  policy planning, 23
  programme planning, 23
  two-fold strategy, 23

Urban poverty, 39–40
Urban problems to be addressed, 92–94
  environmental protection, 93
  informal settlements' retrofitting, 92
  indiscriminate energy consumption, 94
  Lutyen's bungalow area, redensification, 92
  sustainable development, 93
  traffic and transportation management, 93
Urban renewal, 29
  comprehensive renewal, 31
  private and public action, effective cooperation, 31
  private developers and builders, role of, 31
Urban repair, 29
Urban transportation, 27
Urban villages, 42–43
  counterproductive policy, 43
  redevelopment inclusive urban planning, 43
  redevelopment pattern, 43

"Urbanisation of the Earth, The"
  self-contained urban units, 86
US government
  Intermodal Surface Transportation Efficiency Act 1981, 79–80

W

Walkability, 72
Walking, 70–72
Walled city
  Chandni Chowk, 1
  Civil Lines in North, 1–2
  Delhi Cantonment in southwest, 4
  East-West processional way, 2–3
  local identity, 63
  official New Delhi in south, 2
  Rajpath, 2–3
Worker parking, 75–76

103

www.ingramcontent.com/pod-product-compliance
Lightning Source LLC
Chambersburg PA
CBHW051103230426
43667CB00013B/2427